Cambridge Elements ≡

Elements in Theatre, Performance and the Political
edited by
Trish Reid
University of Reading
Liz Tomlin
University of Glasgow

RE-IMAGINING INDEPENDENCE IN CONTEMPORARY GREEK THEATRE AND PERFORMANCE

Philip Hager
Aristotle University of Thessaloniki

CAMBRIDGE
UNIVERSITY PRESS

Shaftesbury Road, Cambridge CB2 8EA, United Kingdom

One Liberty Plaza, 20th Floor, New York, NY 10006, USA

477 Williamstown Road, Port Melbourne, VIC 3207, Australia

314–321, 3rd Floor, Plot 3, Splendor Forum, Jasola District Centre, New Delhi – 110025, India

103 Penang Road, #05–06/07, Visioncrest Commercial, Singapore 238467

Cambridge University Press is part of Cambridge University Press & Assessment, a department of the University of Cambridge.

We share the University's mission to contribute to society through the pursuit of education, learning and research at the highest international levels of excellence.

www.cambridge.org
Information on this title: www.cambridge.org/9781009462303

DOI: 10.1017/9781009250597

First published 2023

A catalogue record for this publication is available from the British Library

ISBN 978-1-009-46230-3 Hardback
ISBN 978-1-009-25057-3 Paperback
ISSN 2753-1244 (online)
ISSN 2753-1236 (print)

Re-imagining Independence in Contemporary Greek Theatre and Performance

Elements in Theatre, Performance and the Political

DOI: 10.1017/9781009250597
First published online: November 2023

Philip Hager
Aristotle University of Thessaloniki
Author for correspondence: Philip Hager, Philip.hager@googlemail.com

Abstract: This Element examines practices that occurred since the beginning of the Greek crisis and revisits the mnemonic canon of the Greek War of Independence. By focusing on the institution of the mnemonic canon of independence, and subsequently on its contemporary re-imaginings, this Element interrogates performance work vis-à-vis Greece's histories of colonial dependencies – histories that are integral to the institution of modern Greece. As such, the examples discussed here rehearse independence against and beyond national(ist) fantasies and, in so doing, attest to an emerging desire for decolonisation.

Keywords: Greece, nation/nationalism, history, crisis, decolonisation

ISBNs: 9781009462303 (HB), 9781009250573 (PB), 9781009250597 (OC)
ISSNs: 2753-1244 (online), 2753-1236 (print)

Contents

Introduction: Imagining Independence

On 25 March 2021, Greece celebrated the bicentenary of the Greek War of Independence – or the 1821 revolution – through which it broke away from the Ottoman Empire and materialised as a nation-state. Celebrations started on 24 March with the grand opening of the renovated National Gallery in Athens and a formal dinner at the Presidential Mansion. The guests of honour represented the three European powers that had assisted the Greek independence effort: the then Prince of Wales and his wife the Duchess of Cornwall, the Russian Prime Minister Mikhail Mishustin and his wife and the French ambassador in lieu of President Emmanuel Macron. In his brief address at the National Gallery Prime Minister, Kyriakos Mitsotakis discussed paintings by Greek and European artists that depict the War of Independence as examples of the cultural affinities between Europe and Greece and emphasised the common stance between Greece and the three European powers in the 'great battles of humanity' over the last two centuries (Hellenic Republic – Prime Minister, 2021).[1] As such, the celebration was unambiguously framed as a reaffirmation of Greece's Europeanness.

As the Greek leadership and its European counterparts celebrated the nation's foundational event by wandering in the centre of the Greek capital, Greeks could only watch the celebrations on the TV due to the strict Covid-19 lockdown regulations implemented by the Greek government. The national body was, thus, absent from the commemoration of the national past, which was to be re-imagined by the European gaze. In other words, while the ailing body of the nation was locked out of sight, this particular re-enactment of national memory drew attention to Greece's uneasy position in the European project: 'a nation forever situated in the interstices of *East* and *West*', as per Stathis Gourgouris's apt phrasing, 'and ideologically constructed by colonialist Europe without ever having been, strictly speaking, colonized' (2021: 6).

The Prime Minister's unwitting *exposé* of Greece's uneasy relationship to Europe – what Michael Herzfeld calls a peculiar 'crypto-colonial' condition (2002) – came in a period of profound economic, social and political crises. Since 2010, Greece has received three bail-out packages that would ostensibly solve its sovereign debt and deficit problems in return for large-scale structural reforms, severe austerity and privatisations.[2] In this context, Greece's GDP has dropped by one-third, privatisations of public assets – including the energy market, seaports, airports and transport – are underway, the overall downsizing of the public sector has accelerated, unemployment rates have risen alarmingly

---

[1] All quotations from Greek sources are translated by me, unless otherwise stated.

[2] For a concise account of the Greek bailout, see Varoufakis (2016: 152–68).

(in 2013 unemployment was at 27.5 per cent) and more than one-third of the population lives in extreme poverty (Pagoulatos, 2018). At the same time, tourism – Greece's 'heavy industry' – was flourishing with tens of millions of visitors each year who were attended to by underpaid and overworked staff; visitors whose presence merely emphasised the inequalities of wealth and further strengthened what Herzfeld calls a 'humiliating dependence [...] on foreign models and power' (Herzfeld, 2016: 56). The promised growth of the economy proved to be a fiction that merely implemented what David Harvey calls 'accumulation by dispossession': the expression of a 'liberal form of imperialism' resulting from 'political unwillingness of the bourgeoisie to give up any of its class privileges' (Harvey, 2004: 69). A fiction, in other words, that rehearsed a neocolonial state of dependency, whereby the troika of creditors – the European Union, European Central Bank and International Monetary Fund – was determining economic and political decisions by indirect and, often, direct interventions.

In response to the escalating economic and political crises, several social movements emerged to reclaim democratic politics, particularly in the first half of the 2010s: the *aganaktismenoi* (indignant) movement that staged people's assemblies in Athens's central square between May and July 2011 is a prominent example. The electoral rise of a coalition of the radical left (SYRIZA) from four to almost 27 per cent in 2012 and to power in 2015 on an anti-austerity platform further marks the disillusionment of the electorate with the political establishment. At the same time, anti-immigration and nationalist rhetoric as well as a state doctrine of intolerance to political dissent permeated mainstream political discourses (Vasilaki and Souvlis, 2021: 21–31). The legitimation of far-right rhetoric is also reflected in the 2012 electoral success of a neo-Nazi party (Golden Dawn) that secured twenty-one seats in the Greek parliament and, subsequently, intensified its street violence. In the same period, finally, increasing numbers of refugees have been attempting the perilous crossing of the Aegean Sea, triggering xenophobic reactions as well as humanitarian responses while also raising ethical questions about Greece and Europe's border-control policies (cf. Cox and Zaroulia, 2016).

Against this backdrop, discussions around independence returned with renewed urgency as some commentators suggested that Greece had become a 'debtors' colony' (Georgiopoulos, 2018), while others spoke about the 'revival of a peculiar cultural colonisation' (Tziovas, 2014; quoted in Tsatsoulis, 2017: 60). Similarly, a growing number of theatre productions have been revisiting the history of the War of Independence thinking through notions of independence again and anew. *Re-imagining Independence in Contemporary Greek Theatre and Performance* examines such practices and more specifically focuses on representations of the 1825–6 siege and exodus of Missolonghi, an event from the Greek War of Independence that, as I discuss in the next section, occupies a central position in its mnemonic canon. How might, I ask, theatre and performance revisit the memory of the nation's foundational moment and re-imagine independence in the present predicament of dependency? How might such performances engage with (the invention of) the national past and enable a process of 'unlearning', as per Ariella Aïsha Azoulay's formulation (2019), so as to re-imagine the communities they inhabit in the present moment? Such questions set the ground upon which the arguments in this Element take shape. But first, it seems imperative to contextualise the Greek War of Independence in the histories and geographies in which it was involved.

The Greek War of Independence in Its Contexts

In *The Age of Revolutions*, Eric Hobsbawm suggests that the 1821 Greek revolution against the Ottoman Empire is part of a wider wave of national revolutions that, inspired by the ideals of the French Revolution, occurred between 1815 and 1848 (1977: 138–9). The early successes of the Greek uprising inspired a wave of international support that mobilised Philhellenism, according to Mark Mazower, 'into an expression of a new kind of politics – international in its range and affiliations, popular in its origins, romantic in its sentiments and often revolutionary in its goals' (2021: 218). This new kind of politics saw volunteer fighters travelling to Greece from all over Europe, committees being set up to gather financial and in-kind support for the Greek cause and artistic works calling the European public to arms by imagining and depicting the horrors of the Greek struggle. In this sense, the philhellenic cause became 'one of the earliest instances of international humanitarian intervention' (Mazower, 2021: 236). This kind of international mobilisation, this 'new kind of politics', was the sign of a rising political subjectivity that would, eventually, shape modern Europe: nationalism.

Paschalis Kitromilides maintains that nationalism was the 'major political force' in the project of modernity, driving European societies' transformation into modern states (2021: 6). The Greek revolution was part of this political milieu even though, as Hobsbawm purports, it stands out as the 'only case [where] the perennial fight of the sheep-herding clansmen and bandit-heroes against *any* real government fuse with the ideas of middle-class nationalism and the French Revolution' (1977: 173). In other words, the Greek War of Independence was envisioned as a national revolution by the (mainly) diasporic bourgeoisie: a mercantile class originating in the Danubian principalities, the Black Sea and the Levant, educated in European capitals and advocating

Enlightenment ideas. Nevertheless, as per Hobsbawm's argument, the war was primarily sustained by the uneducated peasantry of mainland Greece, local chieftains and bandits that, as in other cases in Europe and at least in the beginning of the struggle, hardly exhibited 'any feelings of national conscious-ness, let alone any desire for a national state' (Hobsbawm 1977: 169–70; cf. Mazower, 2021: 326–47). This 'fusion' of discreet political projects joining forces in the Greek War of Independence reflects the complex processes of the imaginary institution of modern Greece – that is, the formation of the Greek subject. It also accounts for the initial disenchantment of European volunteers in the Greek cause who came to realise that the Greek peasantry 'little resembled how they had imagined them' and were reluctant to 'acknowledge that the Greeks too were products of the Ottoman world' (Mazower, 2021: 236); a world that alongside the rest of Balkans was, as Dimitris Tziovas notes, 'invented [. . .] as Europe's "other"' (2003: 2). As the idealisation of the Greeks by the philhellenic cause was tested by actual encounters with them, support for the Greek cause was also questioned. This changed with the fall of Missolonghi in 1826.

After an initial victorious campaign in the first two years of the war, during which the Greeks occupied most of the Peloponnese (the southernmost penin-sula of the mainland), the arrival of Ibrahim Pasha from Egypt in 1824 revital-ised the Ottoman hopes to end the uprising. He soon managed to recapture most of the Peloponnese and contain the Greek insurgents in a small area around Nafplion, the two small islands of Hydra and Spetses, and Missolonghi, a small coastal city in the west of mainland Greece that had endured two sieges between 1822 and 1823. After a third siege that started in the spring of 1825 and lasted for over a year, Ibrahim managed to capture the city in a victory that was supposed to seal the success of his military campaign and end the Greek uprising. Nevertheless, the fierce resistance of the besieged Missolonghites and their subsequent desperate exodus in April 1826, when food and other supplies were becoming increasingly scarce, captured the European liberal imagination. Rather than spelling the end of the Greek war effort, it triggered a sense of 'respectability' while widening the 'social breadth' of sympathy for the Greek cause (Mazower, 2021: 344). Subsequently and against all odds, England, France and Russia entered the war effort and it came down to the naval success of the allied fleet at the bay of Navarino in the Peloponnese in October 1827 to decide the fate of Greek independence.

Missolonghites subsequently emerged in the European imaginary as '"mar-tyrs of the cross" in a clash between Christianity and Islam'. Borrowing the words of Gilbert Heß, Christina Koulouri points out that among philhellenic circles, Missolonghi became a 'synecdoche of the Greek struggle for liberty', connecting 'diverse systems of images and discrete interpretative models' into one 'material topos' (2020: 58). It is for this reason that this Element specifically focuses on contemporary re-imaginings of the events of Missolonghi – because it forms the topography par excellence in the mnemonic canon of the Greek revolution; the landscape in which the Greeks ostensibly performed again and anew their ties to their perceived ancient ancestors. The landscape, conversely, in which Europeans found what, in Friedrich Wilhelm Heinrich Alexander von Humboldt's formulation, was 'that which we ourselves should like to be and produce' (1807 [1963]; quoted in Gourgouris, 2021: 123): a 'sublimated' and colonised, as I will discuss later, Hellenic ideal. But first, it seems crucial to briefly turn to Humboldt's 'we'; that is, the European public.

A European Public

Humboldt's proposition implies a European public that imagines itself as coherent. Yet, who partakes in this imagined community? Where is this European 'we' located? Manuela Boatcă argues that (European) social theory has produced a 'sanitized version of European history that ignores both the experience of the East and the South of Europe, as well as the West's colonial and imperial history' (2021: 390). In this sense, the European public, as articulated by Humboldt and much later by Jürgen Habermas (2012), seems to refer to an imagined European subject of enunciation that is ostensibly coherent and which has been, as per Gurminder K. Bhambra's argument, erected at the back of the colonial project (2022: 241).

Discourses of European unity and singularity are, therefore, founded in the project of colonialism, while perpetually producing, as per Boatcă's proposition, 'a historically consistent politics of difference within Europe that has systematically reproduced the East and the South of Europe as peripheral formations of a Western European core' (2021: 394). In addition, discourses of European unity and singularity 'depend on the silencing of the historical role of its member states and their predecessors in creating the main structures of global political and economic inequality during European colonial rule' (Boatcă, 2021: 395). In other words, Europe's position as the 'wealthiest continent on the planet', as Bhambra maintains, 'is an inheritance that derives from the very same historical processes that have left other places poor' (2022: 240). Europe's politics of difference alongside the processes of silencing and extraction of wealth that are constitutive of the European public are also at work in the making and development of modern Greece. Before the European public, as I discuss in the next section, Greeks have historically appeared under two guises: as celebrated descendants of Europe's ancient ideal and as its deprived epigones, 'forever "catching up" with the West' (Boatcă, 2021: 394), as the Greek crises have demonstrated anew. Or, as Herzfeld has summarised this conundrum that has both motivated and haunted Greeks' nationalisation, Greece is 'a country claiming at once to be the ancestor of Europe and yet also widely seen as one of the continent's newest and least European states' (Herzfeld 2016: 37).

The Nationalisation of the Greeks

The nationalisation of the Greeks entailed, according to Gourgouris, the 'mimicry' of 'an explicit and programmatic *colonization of the [Hellenic] ideal*' by European culture (2021: 124). In this schema, modern Greeks can appear in the European public sphere, as long as they embrace Europe's 'desire', as per Homi Bhabha's conceptualisation of colonial mimicry, 'for a reformed, recognisable Other, as *a subject of difference that is almost the same, but not quite*' (1984: 126). The modern Greek subject, thus, was instituted by way of re-forming into a colonial subject that mimics the European desire for re-discovering its Hellenic roots. This is what Vangelis Calotychos calls a 'discourse of absense' that 'works on its object by a cenotaphic logic', whereby the modern Greek subject remains an empty signifier – a canvas where colonial desire can invent the classical ideal anew (2003: 47).

Central to this process was the work of Adamantios Korais (1748–833), a key figure of modern Greek Enlightenment. Korais's lifelong project of national pedagogy sought to enable an act of transfer, whereby Greek intellectuals ought to 'transfer to the heads of our nation the ripe ideas of the enlightened nations' (1814; quoted in Kotides, 1995: 20). Such an act of transfer, *metakenosis* in Korais's terminology, illustrates in no uncertain terms the aim of his pedagogical project as a Hellenisation of the Greeks. Moreover, it induces, as per Gourgouris's analysis, 'an anxiety of influence' (2021: 92), which places modern Greece at the heart of European imaginings (where it appears as an embodiment of Europe's ancestry), while also consigning the Greek subject to the position of an inadequate Other that can never fully rise to the expectations of its own – and Europe's – genealogy. Or, in Gourgouris's articulation: 'Neohellenic imaginary with the presence of an irretrievable, but permanent, ancestry', which continually produces 'a dogmatically idealized state and its hopelessly inadequate historical rendition' (2021: 152–4). As a consequence of a long-standing 'two-fold colonial gesture', according to Tziovas (2021: 233), this conundrum reflects the dual articulation of colonial mimicry that, in Bhabha's analysis, produces an imitation of the imperial subjectivity and its difference. To paraphrase Bhabha: to be hellenised is emphatically not to be Greek. Or, in the words of Calotychos, 'it is the modern Greek, that "dirty descendant," who disturbs this colonization of space for those who read or appropriate Greek landscape as symbolic capital' (2003: 32). Modern Greeks, as per the European gaze absent from the Hellenic landscape, mimic the colonisation of the ideal by undergoing a process of self-colonisation which, as Calotychos argues, 'works to reinforce a form of cultural, intellectual, and political dependence' (2003: 49).

The claim to ownership of ancient Greek drama is a case in point in relation to this condition of dependence. Dimitris Tsatsoulis suggests that this is part of the 'cultivation of a peculiar kind of Greek nationalism [. . .] by Western Europe. This way [Europe] was "granting" a topos of the western imagination to a specific nation' (2017: 59). Along the same lines, Eleftheria Ioannidou argues that, since the establishment of the Greek nation-state, ancient theatres emerged as national heterotopias, where the Greeks, as the rightful owners of classical heritage, claimed 'exclusive authority over classical antiquity' (2011: 386). Subsequently, performances of classical dramas in ancient theatres 'were expected to propagate the idealized view of modern Greece as an inheritor and successor of classical antiquity' (Ioannidou, 2011: 390). In this sense, even though they claimed ownership of ancient theatres, the Greeks still recognised their indebtedness to the European colonial gaze. Nevertheless, the discussion around the ownership of classical heritage clearly frames the immaterial sphere of cultural production as a commodity and reflects its appropriation by the economic logic of modernity where the value of – material and immaterial – commodities is fundamentally associated with the principle of property. In a very modern sense, therefore, the Greeks have sought to reclaim their assumed cultural identity and tradition by claiming ownership, that is, by affirming their commitment to the cultural and economic logic of European modernity.

Michael Herzfeld suggests that Greece offers a 'most striking case of disemia grounded in the ambiguities of "Europe", at once the spiritual ancestor and, in the early years following accession and once again since crisis struck [. . .] the political pariah of the European Union' (2016: 23). In this sense, the project of nationalisation continually oscillates between an austere neoclassicism fuelled by the anxiety of not appearing European enough and an ostensible Oriental backwardness that meets the Orientalist expectations of the European gaze. If, as per Edward Said's contention, the 'Orient was Orientalized not only because it was discovered to be "Oriental" in all those ways considered commonplace by an average nineteenth-century Europeans, but also because it could be – that is, submitted to being – made Oriental' (2003: 5–6), in modern Greece, the European gaze has found a suitable space of ambivalence, where national imaginings are constantly produced as both European and Oriental; both inside and outside of European imagination but always determined by its gaze.

The War of Independence in the Theatre

In *1821 and the Theatre*, Walter Puchner points out that plays representing the War of Independence and, more generally, historic drama 'contributed to the support and deepening of the national ideology and, often, the national mythology' (2020: 135). Put differently, historic dramas were integral elements to the process of nationalisation. A sub-genre of historic drama that became significant in this respect was 'patriotic drama'; such plays were first published in the build-up to the 1821 uprising, were mainly written by members of the mercantile middle class of the Greek diaspora and, when staged, were performed at educational institutions of the Danubian principalities (Hatzipantazis, 2014: 157–91). In many ways, these early patriotic dramas were carrying out Korais's national pedagogical project. Mostly following the neoclassical tradition, these works echoed Enlightenment ideas and drew their themes from ancient Greece: the past 'that which we ourselves should like to be and produce', as per Humboldt's formulation; the past that would become the inspiration for a national 'awakening'. Later articulations of patriotic drama also included representations of the War of Independence and gradually shifted from neoclassicism to romanticism. The work of Ioannis Zambelios, in many ways rehearsing Korais's national pedagogy, is paradigmatic of early patriotic dramas as it reflects the initial commitment to neoclassicism and the gradual transition to less austere forms, although never quite embracing the romantic aesthetic. Zambelios's work is also exemplary in establishing a connection between the classical world and modern Greeks, something that, according to Anna Tabaki, 'comprises an ideological constant' (2021a: 322). Another example of 'patriotic dramas' was Evanthia Kairi's *Nikiratos* (1826), written in the immediate aftermath of the fall of Missolonghi with which I engage in more detail in Section 1.

Patriotic dramas in the newly formed state increasingly focused on representations from the war. By the second half of the nineteenth century, the production of such dramas was encouraged as part of dramatic contests, while also achieving significant box-office success (Puchner, 2020: 134). As more former Ottoman territories were annexed by the Greek nation-state, such dramas worked to further nationalise the growing population. In the first half of the twentieth century, independence-related patriotic dramas persisted, but their themes also spread to other genres, such as comic and dramatic idyll, comic revues and school plays (Puchner, 2020). As Puchner maintains, the extant production of patriotic dramas and, more generally, the use of patriotic themes coincided with periods of crisis, national disaster or external threat (2020: 133). In the inter-war period, patriotic drama became part of a legitimised cultural milieu and gained 'philosophical depth', rather than serving predominantly nationalist or commercial purposes, as it did in previous periods (Puchner, 2020: 173).

After World War II, representations of the War of Independence became less frequent: changing social, political and economic conditions seem to have reduced the need for plays inspired by the War of Independence (Puchner, 2020: 133). A notable exception was the period of the dictatorship of the colonels (1967–74), when the nationalist regime attempted to capitalise on patriotic drama and, more generally, the use of the national past (cf. Van Steen, 2015 and 2021; Tsoukalas, 2021a and 2021b). Even though this was the case earlier in the post-war years, when the dictatorship ended, there were significant attempts to demystify the national past – perhaps as a result of the dictatorship's ultra-nationalist discourse and use of history. This included, in the immediate post-dictatorship years, subversive revivals of nineteenth-century plays that dealt with issues of national identity as well as new plays representing the War of Independence. An important example of the latter is Vassilis Ziogas's *The Bottle*, written in 1973 and staged in 1979; it created an absurdist universe for the re-telling of the events of Missolonghi. Another example was Andreas Staikos's 1991 play *1843*, which revolved around the ways in which certain members of the emerging Greek bourgeoisie capitalised on their participation in the war for personal gain. The return of the War of Independence on the Greek stages after 2010, finally, can be partly justified as a build-up to the celebrations of the bicentennial, but, as I propose in this Element, it is mainly a consequence of the condition of the crisis that exposed Greece's foundational dependency anew. As I discuss in Sections 2, 3 and 4, rather than questioning the use of the national past by the state, performances between 2010 and 2021 seemed to problematise its national institution.[3] They seem, in other words, to rethink independence within what Lina Rosi calls a 'post-national' framework that extends beyond history's incarceration in the 'official closed narratives' of the nation (Rosi, 2021).

As a conclusion to the aforementioned brief account of the history of stage representations of the War of Independence in modern Greece, it is important to place patriotic and historic dramas within the national theatrical canon. The works that form this canon are not uniform; they employ a wide range of representational strategies and belong to different genres. What is common in these works is their consistent observation of the constant re-making of national

---

[3] Apart from the examples discussed in this book, I indicatively mention some productions that are relevant to the discussions in this book: *Dance me to the End of Greece: Foreign Travelers in Greece*, by Kyriaki Spanou (Benaki Museum, 2012); *Athanasios Diakos: The Return*, by Lena Kitsopoulou (Athens Festival, 2012); *Golfo*, by Spiridon Peresiades (National Theatre, 2013, dir. Nikos Karathanos); *Golfo*, by Spiridon Peresiades (six versions between 2004and 2014, dir. Simos Kakalas); *Haiti, a Performance about History* (HATARI theatre group, 2016); *The Woman from Zakynthos*, by Dionisios Solomos (Municipal Theatre of Piraeus, 2021, dir. Antzela Brouskou); *1821, the Revue*, by Dimitris Karantzas and Foivos Delivorias (Municipal Theatre of Piraeus, 2021); *A Country Two Centuries Later*, by Andreas Flourakis (Dodoni Festival/Municipal Theatre of Kozani/Anima theatre company, 2021).

subjects and, as such, their participation in this process (cf. Hatzipantazis, 2014). In studying and, to a certain degree, delineating this canon, theatre historiography has often produced modern Greek theatre history as part of a linear movement towards an inevitable national completion (cf. Tabaki, 1993 and 1997; Hatzipantazis, 2014; Puchner, 2020). Important as this approach may be in tracing the parallel development of a national theatrical tradition and national identities, here I am interested in the national canon as part of a wider web of cultural practices involved in the institution of modern Greece – a set of performative acts of transfer that produce as much as document the institution of Greekness vis-à-vis the transformations of Greek society; practices that constitute a scenario that produces modern Greece each time it is rehearsed – every time again and anew. I call this the scenario of independence.

Methodological Considerations: Scenarios as Containers of Memory

I borrow the term 'scenario' from Diana Taylor's *The Archive and the Repertoire: Performing Cultural Memory in the Americas* (2003), and I am particularly interested in the ways in which, as an analytic strategy, it enables the study of archival documents in tandem with performative repertoires. Scenarios, as Taylor proposes, operate as 'meaning-making paradigms that structure social environments, behaviors, and potential outcomes' (Taylor, 2003: 28). They work, in other words, as containers of cultural knowledge and memory and institute communities as they are enacted by them – each time again and anew. If archival documents are presumably durable, the repertoire 'both keeps and transforms choreographies of meaning' (Taylor, 2003: 20). And it is the durability of the document – which ostensibly contains unalterable knowledge that has to be discovered – in conjunction with the malleability of the repertoire – which requires the presence of the community to be produced again and anew – that allows scenarios to both reproduce and resist dominant narratives and discourses within a given social environment. A scenario does not imitate the event it commemorates but re-activates it by way of including spectators in its frame and 'implicating' them 'in its ethics and politics' (Taylor, 2003: 33). A scenario, thus, is fluid: it changes, it slips and it adapts.

Taylor discusses the act of the 'discovery of America' as constitutive of the 'scenario of discovery' that imposes a gaze whose scope determines 'universal' knowledge. The scenario of discovery 'constructs the wild object and the viewing subject – producing a "we" and "our" as it produces a "them"' (2003: 54). Similarly, Azoulay discusses the operation of the photographic shutter 'as a synecdoche for the operation of the imperial enterprise altogether' (2019: 2): each repetition of its movement reproduces the imperial logic in much the same way that each repetition of the scenario of discovery expands the colonial project; repetition fragments, dissects and exploits new worlds. The technology of photography, in this context, corresponds to an imperial technology of seeing, not the technical innovation that created the actual photographic shutter; a technology that creates a field of visibility and a privileged gaze by arranging imperial time and space and organising the body-politic of the empire. This field of visibility – consisting of de-territorialised worlds, gestures, resources and subjectivities – forms imperial history as universal and driven by the constant pursuit of progress (Azoulay, 2019: 18); history as the repetitive and expansive movement of the photographic shutter that, much like the scenario of discovery, rehearses colonial appropriation and the subsequent ruination of 'new' worlds.

What I call the scenario of independence works in similar ways to the scenario of discovery – in that Greece was the object of re-discovery by the European gaze. According to Tziovas, Greece has been re-discovered several times between the late eighteenth century and the present moment (2021: 233–48). The final re-discovery, ostensibly encapsulating all previous ones, occurred in the beginning of the crises when Greeks were at once exoticised, vilified, victimised and idealised by the European gaze (Tziovas, 2021: 236–42). The scenario of independence differs from the scenario of discovery inasmuch as Greece as the object of discovery is – or needs to become – a projection of the viewing subject's imagining of itself: should Greeks perform the act of self-colonisation as discussed earlier, they can be re-discovered as independent by the European public – they can enter the field of visibility of the imperial shutter. In the context of the crisis, this act of self-colonisation also recalls what Maurizio Lazzarato calls the '"morality" of debt [that] results in the moralization of the unemployed, the "assisted," the users of public services, as well as of entire populations' (2012: 30). It is through discourses that invented the 'lazy Greeks' against north Europeans that 'slave away under gloomy skies for the good of Europe and humanity' that this morality operates (Lazzarato, 2012: 30–1). It follows that guilt – the product of the morality of debt – forced the indebted Greeks to demonstrate their commitment to the integrity of the European project in order to regain the confidence of global capitalism's institutions and become credible debtors – to be discovered again as European partners. Yet, in such a project, independence is predicated on their repeated performances of dependence.

Unlearning Independence

Re-imagining Independence in Contemporary Greek Theatre and Performance does not offer an exhaustive study of the scenario of independence and its contemporary iterations; it does not seek to fully map the history of the transformations of Greek national memory or deliver a detailed analysis of the resurgence of political theatre in Greece during the crisis (cf. Arfara, 2016: 73–115). Rather, it seeks to trace the ways in which Greek theatre practitioners might gesture towards a de-colonising project: I am particularly interested in the ways in which the scenario of independence has been re-imagined in the last decade by what Maria Boletsi and Dimitris Papanikolaou call a 'critical opening which starts by destabilising a long line of idealized mappings' (Boletsi and Papanikolaou, 2022: 134). Indeed, the examples discussed in this Element emerge as part of a wider trend in contemporary Greek theatre that seems to challenge the idealised figure of the Hellene and, in doing so, re-position Greece in the European and Global South; to unlearn, in other words, their commitment to the European public and re-imagine independence by learning from (their positioning in) the South that, according to Boaventura de Sousa Santos, is 'a metaphor for the systematic suffering inflicted upon large populations by Western-centric colonialism, capitalism and patriarchy' (2020: 35). Even though the process of Hellenisation and the idealised mappings it produced seemed to obscure such systematic suffering, Greeks as Europe's epigones have perpetually experienced it – the ongoing crises being the most recent case.

In pursuing this argument, Section 1 traces the origins of the scenario of independence by looking at the nineteenth-century visual and theatrical representations that compose Missolonghi's mnemonic canon. Focusing on three paintings (Eugene Delacroix's *Greece on the Ruins of Missolonghi* and Theodoros Vryzakis's *The Exodus of Missolonghi* and *The Reception of Lord Byron at Missolonghi*) that present their independence-related themes in strikingly theatrical arrangements and a play (Evanthia Kairi's patriotic drama *Nikiratos*), I demonstrate the ways in which such representations rely on and perform the European gaze. In Sections 2, 3 and 4 I turn to three contemporary performances – Aris Biniaris's *'21* (Athens Festival, 2015), Eleni Efthymiou's rendition of Dionisios Solomos's *The Free Besieged* (2023 Eleusis European Cultural Capital, 2021) and Anestis Azas's *The Republic of Baklava* (Athens Festival, 2021), which unsettle the scenario by re-imagining independence beyond the national register and the aesthetic traditions and representational structures implicated in it. The Coda, finally, turns to performances of the national body and, in doing so, considers the nationalisation of the body-politic by focusing on repertoires rehearsed by members of the Greek Presidential Guard in juxtaposition to Pantelis Flatsousis's *National Fashion-Show* (Athens Festival, 2021).

The performance examples discussed in this Element were staged in prestigious institutions, namely the Athens and Epidaurus Festival and the Eleusis 2023 European Capital of Culture. As such, questions about their efficacy in disrupting dominant iterations of the scenario of independence, while participating and being funded by the very institutions they sought to challenge, might be disputed. Similar questions might also be addressed in relation to the audiences who might have attended those productions – by and large educated and liberal audiences. Such interrogation of the frameworks in which these productions were hosted must be acknowledged. Nevertheless, since the beginning of the crisis, funding for Greek theatres has been scarce: state funding was suspended between 2010 and 2017, and such festivals, alongside private cultural institutions, have been the only places outside of the commercial circuit where practitioners could do paid work (cf. Hager, 2017). Moreover, even though state funding has resumed, these festivals offer wider visibility both inside and outside the Greek borders. Regardless of the audiences who attended these shows, therefore, I focus on the selected examples as they reveal a tendency within the field of theatre that intersects with other practices both inside and outside of the border. What interests me, in other words, is not whether the invitation they extend is efficacious or whether their audiences are already prone to accept it but the invitation itself as a manifestation of a growing political subjectivity.

'Imagine that the origins of photography are not to be found somewhere around the beginning of the nineteenth century [. . .]. Imagine that those origins go back to 1492. What could this mean?' (Azoulay 2019: 2–3). Azoulay's invitation to imagine a 'potential history' of photography by way of 'unlearning the knowledge of the experts' (2019: 3) is the starting point of a strategy of 'unlearning imperialism [that] involves different types of "de-," such as decompressing and decoding; "re-," such as reversing and rewinding; and "un-," such as unlearning and undoing' (Azoulay 2019: 10). Unlearning imperialism rehearses a 'principle of reversibility of what should have not been possible' (Azoulay 2019: 10). Rewinding does not entail nostalgia for an 'idyllic' past; it is not a return to an 'authentic' pre-colonial past but a refusal to accept imperial history as universal and its violence as natural (2019: 56). A central argument pursued in this Element is that the mnemonic strategies employed in the performances discussed here correspond, although in very different ways, to such a project of unlearning by way of re-imagining independence through the contemporary experience of the different facets of the Greek crises, that is, by way of re-imagining independence beyond and against the imperial field of visibility.

The imperial field of visibility is the domain of the archive: photography, after all, seeks to capture the present moment. The logic of the imperial shutter, therefore, works in similar ways to the logic of the archive that, as per Jacques Derrida's discussion, resides in a 'place of election where law and singularity intersect in *privilege*' (1998: 3). The archive, he continues, contains 'an impression' of history as instituted by authority and archival technology determines not 'merely the moment of the conservational record-ing, but rather the very institution of the archivable event' (1998: 18). The archive, therefore, produces events and their documents in its own image – the image of authority; it produces imperial history as both lived experience and memory. The productions discussed here use different fragments of the archive of the War of Independence. In doing so, they engage with the 'promise of the documentary', which, according to Janelle Reinelt, 'is to provide access or connection to reality through the facticity of documents, but not without creative mediation, and individual and communal spectator-ial desire' (2009: 22–3).

In mediating the archive of history, the performances produced renewed encounters with history as much as they invoked images and experiences from contemporary Greece with a renewed sense of historicity. Such treatment of the archive chimes with Dimitris Papanikolaou's conceptualisation of 'arch-ive trouble', which seeks to '"unearth" hidden voices or lost patterns' while 'problematiz[ing] the process of unearthing and digging' (2017: 47). It is not only a matter of making the invisible visible but of highlighting the notion that no archive can ever be complete. In this way, Papanikolaou continues, it 'also attacks the inconsistency of ideologies anchoring their legitimacies to grand narratives and "settled" archival records' (2017: 48). Rather than aspiring to provide an authentic account of the historical events, the productions discussed here seek to unsettle national history, that is, to de-stabilise the archive by adapting or reframing the performative repertoires of the War of Independence. In this sense, I propose that these contemporary re-imaginings of the scenario of independence perform archive trouble inasmuch as they challenge the promise of the documentary and, in doing so, perform gestures of unlearning imperial history.

1 Missolonghi and the Scenario of Independence

The Exodus from Missolonghi (1853), a painting by Theodoros Vryzakis, the 'illustrator par excellence of the [Greek] Revolution' (Mykoniatis, 1995: 13), depicts the moment when the defenders of Missolonghi attempted their exodus (see Figure 1). Bathed in light, the Greeks are crossing a wooden drawbridge under the watchful gaze of Jesus Christ and his angels. They are awaited by the Ottoman soldiers – dark figures standing with arms raised in the darkness. On the drawbridge, two lovers share their last kiss; under it, two mothers try to protect their infant children – one of them might already be dead. Back on the drawbridge, some Greek fighters are wounded, with their suffering clearly

Figure 1 Vryzakis Theodoros (Thebes 1814 or 1819 – Munich 1878), *The Exodus from Missolonghi* (1853), Oil on canvas, 169 × 127 cm, Π.5446, © National Gallery – Alexandros Soutsos Museum, Photography Stavros Psiroukis

reflected in their eyes, while others look upon them with sorrow – pain and determination are drawn on their faces in equal amounts. In contrast, the besiegers move towards the city walls unconcerned about their own losses or the suffering of the enemy. '[W]e could almost hear the noise of weapons and the cries of the wounded', reads the description of the painting in the National Gallery in Athens – 'the painter has depicted the scene in great accuracy and meticulousness' (National Gallery, 2022). Indeed, it appears that the particular work captures the pathos of that iconic scene from the Greek War of Independence.

Taking into account that the painting was created almost three decades after the event by someone who was not a direct witness, however, one should ask: what do words such as 'accuracy' and 'meticulousness' mean? Or, rather, one should consider the function of this painting within the representational canon of the war: might such a description not imply that the painting is a historical document that, as per the National Gallery's phrasing, 'evokes one of the most renowned and tragic episodes in the Greek struggle for independence' (National Gallery, 2022)? Vryzakis's painting, thus, implicitly introduces the key issues and questions discussed in this section. It is a case in point when thinking of the representational canon of the war: it captures the key elements of the mythologisation of Missolonghi as a 'sacred city' and, by the same token, constitutes a document of the scenario of independence. At the same time, it enables us to consider the distinction between the past and its narration, offering itself as an illustration of the operation of national ideology towards the institution of national memory and the subjects practicing it. Might this painting, in other words, not evoke the memory of the event rather than the event itself and, in doing so, devise a way to interpret it?

Let us briefly return to Vryzakis's painting. There are two main binary oppositions at work in this image: the first one is between the 'civilised' Greeks who are bathed in light and are presented in some emotional and psychological depth and the 'barbaric' Ottomans who stand in the dark and in whose representation, there is little, if any, emotional or narrative depth – they are dehumanised. This opposition between civilisation and barbarity can also be articulated as the opposition between Christianity and Islam and, by extension, Europe and the Orient. The second opposition, 'liberty or death', is depicted with an almost brutal realism and constitutes the central speech act driving the Greek struggle for independence. In terms of the mnemonic canon, this speech act is at once a revolutionary maxim that inspired the Greek independence fighters and a container that 'condenses', as per Koulouri's analysis, a series of interpretative strategies of the War of Independence (2020: 59). In this sense, the two binary oppositions converge to reaffirm that, on a discursive level, liberty is identified with Europe and death is the domain of the Orient. In addition, Vryzakis's painting visualises the central embodied repertoire of the exodus: the procession, the walk and the bodies moving in concert – equally religious and secular. Thus, in this iteration of the scenario, the exodus is idealised and aestheticised: in the performance of the procession, the onlooker is invited to witness not the fall of Missolonghi but the institution of Greek independence on the firm foundations of Christianity, humanism and Europeanness.

Philhellenic Visions

Koulouri maintains that the European interest in the Greek cause was, initially at least, constructed on two pillars, both of which precede the War of Independence in the European imaginary: the liberation of the remains of classical antiquity from the 'barbarians' and a sense of Christian solidarity against a common enemy (Koulouri, 2020: 48). It was their supposed ancestry and shared religion that mattered and Greek independence was, in this sense, something that the European gaze imagined regardless, or in the absence of modern Greeks. This absence is particularly striking in pre-revolutionary travelogues of philhellenes, in which, as Gourgouris points out, amongst the abundance of classical ruins, 'whatever life the modern Greeks may have had becomes invisible; the traveler's pen (or camera) will rub them off' (2021: 131).

After 1821, however, the spectacle of the Greek War of Independence was disseminated in the European public sphere. As Koulouri proposes:

> Western societies' interest to the Greek Revolution corresponded to the ever-growing curiosity of [European] urban dwellers for places they had yet to visit and most probably would never do so; representations of events they had not experienced and of extraordinary figures they had not met. Modern forms of entertainment that started developing from the end of the eighteenth century onwards target urban populations who, in turn, seek pleasure in spectacles that commercialise history (Koulouri, 2020: 50)

As the Greek war effort mounted the European stages and entered the European houses, therefore, the social breadth of the appetite for images from the Greek War of Independence outgrew the liberal philhellenic circles: the urban bourgeoisie that, rather than or apart from being committed to the cause, was merely seeking a few hours of escapism into a world of images that, for them, lay between reality and representation – between sympathy for the struggle of the Greeks and an Orientalist thirst to look at the Other. In this sense, the technologies of industrialisation and its cultural logic that seeks to visualise – and thus to colonise – history seemed to favour the Greeks, even more so as the iconography of the war entered the quotidian realm through a series of domestic and everyday objects – chinaware, playing cards, tablecloths and clothing among others – decorated with events, faces and landscapes of the war. There was a liquor called Missolonghi and 'Missolonghi grey' became a fashionable colour for men's trousers (Koulouri, 2020: 51–2).

Underlying this 'philhellenic emporium', as per Austrian chancellor Klemens von Metternich's ironic pronouncement (Koulouri, 2020: 51), was a deeper and more pressing political opposition between liberals that sought to revive republicanism and conservatives whose commitment to the European status quo was unwavering. One of the most striking aspects of the new kind of politics pushed forward by Philhellenism, as Mazower maintains, was the 'consciousness of a European public and its political significance' (2021: 234). In this context, the London philhellenic committee, for instance, worked towards securing loans for the revolutionary Greek administration. It also recruited Lord George Gordon Byron to lead an expedition to Greece. Byron's arrival in Missolonghi in January 1824 lent legitimacy to the Greek war effort while also helping to temporarily resolve internal tensions within the Greek revolutionary administration. His death a few months later in Missolonghi was, as Mazower notes, 'a sensation across Europe' (2021: 260) and consolidated the position of the Greek cause within the frames of visibility in the continent.

Against this backdrop, the French Comité Grec organised a collective exhibition for the benefit of the Greeks that opened in May 1826 at Gallerie Lebrun in Paris with contributions from major contemporary artists, including several works by Jacques-Louis David, who had recently died in exile. If volunteers in the early years of the war represent, as per Mazower's phrasing, a 'humanitarian intervention' on the ground, the Lebrun exhibition, as Tom Prideaux maintains, was the 'first time painters had acted together so solidly for a humanitarian cause' (1966: 79). The liberal press responded with enthusiasm to the artists' readiness to support the Greek cause, particularly because, as noted in the *Revue Encyclopédique*, history

> will not fail to compare the attitude of peoples with that of governments, and to point out that, whereas in the past the whole of Europe has often risen at the call of its kings and priests to march in rescue of other Christians, this time the thrones and the altars have remained silent (1826; quoted in Athanassoglou-Kallmyer, 1989: 39)

Contrary to this position, the conservative *Gazette de France* condemned the intentions behind the exhibition as unconvincing 'philanthropic grimaces of the revolutionaries, Bonapartists, imperialists who are all more or less skilfully disguised under the general denomination of Liberals' (1826; in Athanassoglou-Kallmyer, 1989: 40). The exhibition was, they purported, liberal propaganda which had found in Philhellenism, a new battlefield against the status quo: 'Yesterday it was the issue of blacks; today the Greeks are the talk of the town; the negrophiles [sic] have been transformed into philhellenes' (1826; quoted in Athanassoglou-Kallmyer, 1989: 40–1). This exhibition, it appears, exposed political tensions rising in Europe in the first half of the nineteenth century and the position of the Greek question in them (cf. Drakopoulou, 2021: 33–64). The fall of Missolonghi, just weeks before the opening of the exhibition, accelerated the processes through which liberal politics would eventually gain momentum, and this is also evident in the large number of paintings and other artworks that sought to depict the event (cf. Athanssoglou-Kallmyer, 1989: 66–107).[4]

A significant work that participated in a renewed version of the Lebrun exhibition that opened in the summer of 1826 was Eugene Delacroix's *Greece on the Ruins of Missolonghi* (1826). In the foreground stands a pale female figure, Greece, with her chest partly exposed. She is kneeling on the rubble of the fallen city with her hands stretching down by the sides of her body and her palms open in a gesture of submission and, perhaps, supplication. Her gaze is directed to a point outside the frame of the painting. Behind her, at the top right corner of the frame, a dark-skinned Ottoman raises victoriously the 'standard of the crescent', while observing the ruins of the conquered city that lay behind the figure of Greece. This was not the first time that Delacroix drew inspiration from the Greek struggle for independence as can be documented by his 1824 painting *The Massacre at Chios*. In this case, the scene consists of injured Greeks captured by Ottoman soldiers at the forefront, while at the back lie ruins. Delacroix's response to the 1822 massacre at Chios seems to offer a fairly realistic – even if romanticised – account of the events, while his response to the fall of Missolonghi was an allegory. In relation to the latter, Mazower suggests that 'Greece be depicted as a defenceless woman, in need of Europe's aid, was nothing new [. . .]. What was new was the political context – for a defenceless woman was now a call to arms' (2021: 333).[5] Nevertheless, Delacroix's call to arms needs to be read keeping in mind the Orientalist gaze that lies at the heart of this representation of Greece.

Mazower maintains that '[t]here was an inescapable racial dimension to the outcry as well. It was not only that the Greeks were Christians, not that they

---

[4] Such mobilisation of the European public that, while focusing on a specific (humanitarian) cause elsewhere, operates as a means to address intra-European political tensions and conflicts is not uncommon in European history. One could also suggest that Europe's responses to the current Greek crises are part of the same milieu: the Greeks became at once the prodigal child of the European family – as per the conservative perspective – and the paradigm of resistance to the neoliberal order – as per the liberal argument. As such, discussions around the Greek crisis were by and large thinly covered excuses for wider debates around the neoliberal restructuring of the world and, more specifically, the EU.

[5] One could also argue here that Greece's female presence calling the people to rise against an oppressive order is reminiscent of his later depiction of Liberty in *Liberty Leading the People* (1830) that sought to commemorate the July 1830 revolution in Paris. Yet, while both paintings are calls to arms, Liberty appears as a much more commanding figure – not a supplicant as Greece but a revolutionary force.

represented a link to the classical past the Europe so prized. It was also that their captors were Muslims and Africans' (2021: 338). This racialised opposition between Europe and the Orient is striking in Delacroix's painting, as was in the earlier depiction of the massacre at Chios – both works are structured around the juxtaposition between figures of classical whiteness bathed in light- and dark-skinned Oriental figures standing in the dark. Critic Boutard's words clearly demonstrate how such a racialised opposition was (to be) received: 'in the distance a negro [*sic*] raising the standard of the crescent over the ruins of Greece, evokes the idea of the country of Miltiades and Pericles now reduced to be the slave of a slave' (1826; quoted in Athanassoglou-Kallmyer, 1989: 92). The black body appears as cause for alarm and, accordingly, the white body, which may take on further significations – an allusion to virgin Mary, for example – is the eternal symbol of purity and innocence. This idealisation of Greece and denigration of her enemies is, thus, an expression of the European Orientalist gaze: first, the racial difference that reduces the non-white body to a 'slave', as per Boutard's configuration; second, the absence of the Greek bodies from the scene, which is compensated by the symbolic presence of the female body of Greece – a body, nevertheless, that is not representing Greece as much as it re-invents it as per the European philhellenic colonisation of the Hellenic ideal. Delacroix, therefore, plays within a well-rehearsed scenario of philhellenic imagery, whereby, as Nina Athanassoglou-Kallmyer notes, '[p]ersonifications of a desperate Greece [were commonly] surrounded by the remains of her illustrious past' (1989: 97). The ways in which the Orientalist gaze played out the conflict in the European public sphere becomes apparent and it concerns both sides: if the 'barbarians' were non-white, Muslim and slaves by default, the 'civilised' should appear white, Christian, pure and somehow connected to classical Greece. This reductive and formulaic account of the Greek War of Independence lies at the foundations of the scenario of independence.

Sébastien Allard and Côme Fabre dismiss early critics' comments on Greece's state and stance that she is agitated or afraid. Instead, they suggest that she 'seems to accept as ineluctable the sacrifice imposed on her as she exhibits her wounds to the viewer' (Allard and Côme, 2018: 71) or, as Athanassoglou-Kallmyer notes, her gaze is one of 'sad reproach [...] meant to awaken the emotions' (1989: 100). While in the first reading, she becomes a symbol of the fall of civilisation with a hint of supplication towards those who partake in the same cultural milieu, the latter analysis presents Greece as a judge of those who have failed her and forced her to become a sacrificial lamb. In either case, Delacroix's call to arms produces Greece as a ragged and helpless woman, who may or may not be in distress; a woman, nevertheless, who is certainly reproachful of her state that does not align with her glorious past. In such a discursive formulation, Greece can only participate in the European imaginary as someone in need of protection from the barbarous world that has engulfed her (assumed) past glories. What follows is that the opposition between civilisation and barbarity does not include Greeks at all – it is an opposition between the European colonising gaze and its non-European imperial counterpart. Even though Greece became highly visible, through its colonised image, Greeks remained invisible.

Evanthia Kairi's *Nikiratos*

Another 'call to arms' that was produced in the immediate aftermath of the fall of Missolonghi was Evanthia Kairi's *Nikiratos*. Kairi, 'one of the most prominent women writers of Greece's revival' (Mpalanos, 1930; quoted in Stivanaki, 2000: 257), conceived *Nikiratos* as a '"written exposé" in three acts of the events of Missolonghi' (Stivanaki, 2000: 260).[6] According to Puchner, *Nikiratos* observes the general mannerisms of the classicist model – the unities of time, place and plot, and it includes a chorus of women and no more than three characters ever appear on stage at once (Puchner, 2020: 366). Yet, its patriotic fervour and the way in which certain dilemmas operate as dramaturgical drives or the use of other devices veer towards romantic drama (Puchner, 2020: 367). This 'lack of stylistic coherence' is not, according to Puchner, weakening the whole: true to the demands of patriotic drama, 'the narration of events is deemed more important than the artful negotiation of dramatic form' (2020: 338).

The play begins on the evening before the exodus, when the city's garrison has made the decision for the desperate act if the supplies that are on the way are unable to reach the city. Nikiratos, the head of the garrison, cannot bring himself to leave the besieged city but does not wish his children to stay as well. As the supplies are captured by the enemy, they attempt the exodus, which, due to an act of treason, fails. Missolonghi's conqueror Ibrahim enters the city for the first time just before Nikiratos's return for a final patriotic speech. The play ends with Nikiratos setting the city and everyone who is in it ablaze.

A key conflict driving the play's dramaturgy aside from the war effort is between Nikiratos and his daughter Kleoniki: early in the first act, the daughter

---

[6] The text was published anonymously in Nafplion in July 1826, and in 1827, author Alexandros Soutsos 'dare[d] to declare [Kairi] as its mother and place her among the chorus of the Muses' (Soutsos, 1827; quoted in Tabaki, 2021b: 40). According to Tambaki, there is evidence of the play being staged in Syros in 1827 for an audience of refugees from the mainland and in Athens in 1837, but its first recorded performance was in 1838 in Missolonghi (2021b: 40). It can be assumed, therefore, that although it was written for the stage, it was first read rather than watched.

announces her determination to remain, against her father's wish, in Missolonghi in the case of an exodus:

> Is it not better [for a woman] to die in freedom for her [motherland] with what is most dear in the world, than to wander here and there not knowing where to turn, and to risk times and again losing her valuable freedom, for which she has suffered so much? (Kairi, 2021: 23)

By committing to the national cause, Kleoniki's wilful refusal to abandon the city complicates the play's narrative in that it questions her father's authority over her own right to self-determination. This conflict reaches its climax and is resolved at the end of the second act where Nikiratos comes to terms with Kleoniki's request and recognises that he shares the same destiny with his two children. This sub-plot serves to shift the focus onto Kleoniki, setting her as an example to Greek women, who should claim an equal share in the war effort by sacrificing themselves alongside the men.

Puchner proposes a reading of Kleoniki in conjunction with the play's introductory letter 'to Greek women', which demonstrates the play's didactic function as an 'advisory act of encouragement toward the correct stance of women in the struggle' (Puchner, 2020: 343). This is further emphasised by Kairi's dedication to 'the women that sacrificed their lives for Greece' (Kairi, 2021: 13). Evanthia Stivanaki maintains that *Nikiratos* was Kairi's 'own contribution to the case of the motherland' (2000: 261). Kleoniki's presence and specific stance in such a central position in the play's dramaturgy, therefore, constitutes a call to women to place their allegiance to the nation above their allegiance to their family and to act in any way they can in the interests of national independence. Stivanaki also proposes that the character of Nikiratos directly references Christos Kapsalis, one of the leaders of Missolonghi, but is also 'vested with the virtues of [Kairi's] brother Theofilos Kairis', a leading figure in Greek Enlightenment (2000: 261–2). Accordingly, 'in Kleoniki [Kairi] demarcated herself as dramatic character' (2000: 264), thereby symbolically introducing herself as an active agent in the War of Independence. In this sense, her decision to write and publish *Nikiratos* as a performative declaration – a speech act – of her commitment to the cause is also her way of acting in the war.

Nevertheless, Nikiratos remains the main producer of discourse in this play. His interlocutors often operate as mouthpieces that enable his fiery patriotic diatribes that offer a discursive framing for the histories in which the actions of the characters participate. His meeting with Ibrahim's European envoy in the first act is exemplary in this respect. The envoy offers a final opportunity to Missolonghi's garrison to surrender and is met with nothing but disdain: 'the

Turk will not find joy [in Missolonghi]; you will not find joy, you who have become Mehmet [Ali]'s slaves for a little gold' (Kairi, 2021: 28). Nikiratos, thus, embarks on his first tirade that separates the stance of 'the real friends of Greece [who] did not come to her for prizes and rewards' from those Europeans who, much like the envoy himself, 'came for the ignoble silver [and who], not finding what they hoped, left us and were not ashamed to help and guide the Turks' (Kairi, 2021: 29). In his next diatribe, Nikiratos distinguishes the diasporic Greeks who have not aided the struggle from those who gave everything to the struggle, 'only to see the Greek nation being politically educated' (Kairi, 2021: 31). He then talks about the Greek nation 'whose ancestors educated the world and which [. . .] preserved its national character' (Kairi, 2021: 31). Moreover, Greeks presented the first obstacle in the Ottomans' way into Europe and through their 'sacrifice, impeded them [Ottomans] from devouring the rest of Europe' (Kairi, 2021: 31). Not only are the Greeks Europe's ancestors, but they were also its saviours, which further strengthens Greece's plea to Europe. The final speech returns to the European response to the war and poses a question: 'which European monarch, should they learn the real predicaments of the Greeks, should they glimpse at Missolonghi for a single moment, would not immediately decide to offer their help?' (Kairi, 2021: 33).

In this scene, Kairi outlines the contexts in which the Greek War of Independence is fought while also proposing a way of looking at these contexts that reproduces philhellenic rhetoric, and, by virtue of this, it lays the foundations of Greek exceptionalism by emphasising a historical recurrence of national suffering. Nikiratos's speeches also rehearse the 'Hellenisation of Greek history' that later legitimised the Greek nation-state as the continuation of the classical world and whose institutional expression was Konstantinos Paparigopoulos's *History of the Modern Greek Nation* (1860–76) that 'structured Greek national time as an uninterrupted continuum' (Plantzos, 2016: 41). Framed in this way, the Greek claim to independence exposes Europe's ostensible debts to the Greeks while also fully adopting the European desire to rediscover Greece. What is implied in this claim to independence, therefore, is that it can only be achieved if Europe desires it or, conversely, that there is an implicit acceptance (or even advocacy) of a different kind of dependency on European colonial power. This play, then, is as much addressed to Greek women, as per Kairi's dedication, as it is directed to the European public. It is a display of suffering and self-sacrifice as much as it is the presentation of the Greeks' Hellenisation.

This is further emphasised if one looks at the names of the characters. Stivanaki maintains that ancient Greek names demarcate the 'positive' characters (as opposed to the anonymous European and Ibrahim that are considered 'negative' characters) and, furthermore, establish a conception of national continuity (Stivanaki, 2000: 267). Accordingly, Nikiratos and Kleoniki are linked to victory – *niki* means victory – and Lysimachus, the garrison's lieutenant, is the catalyst of the battle – *lisis* and *mache* mean solution and battle, respectively. Puchner suggests that Kairi's care towards the 'positive characters [. . .] transforms their holocaust into victory' (2020: 341). As useful as such an analytical approach might be in implicitly establishing a discursive connection between the modern Greeks and their idealised predecessors alongside the binary opposition of civilisation vs. barbarity, I propose a slightly different reading: what seems crucial here is that the ancient Greek names in the nineteenth-century Missolonghi are not simple linguistic signs but performative utterances that rehearse a 'resurrection' of the ancient nation fighting for its independence. This constitutes a performative gesture that seems to make a case before the European public that the Greek nation stands apart from the Ottoman world and is ready to claim its historical destiny, that is, ready to be re-discovered and, as such, re-invented by the European gaze.

Much like Delacroix's *Greece on the Ruins of Missolonghi*, *Nikiratos* was a call to arms. Like Delacroix's painting, Kairi's play was written within three months of the fall of the Missolonghi, at a moment when the possibility of independence seemed distant. Both these works, then, were created with no knowledge, no hindsight and with very little optimism for the outcome of the war. In tracing *Nikiratos*'s patriotic agenda alongside (or due to) its European influences, most studies seem to regard it with the determinism they are afforded by their historical vantage point – as if *Nikiratos* was written with a view to document the future success of the Greek struggle. Stivanaki, for example, proposes that *Nikiratos* is a play with 'elements and intentions of "historical documentary"', while the events narrated in it 'serve as a sufficient and necessary condition for the construction of macro-historical symbolisms, perceptions, moral stances and values' (2000: 261–2). Thus, *Nikiratos* is understood as both a historical document of the war and its retrospective commemoration from a future that appears as already determined in 1826. Rather than an event documenting the success of the war effort, I approach *Nikiratos* as an event – an intervention – in the war itself, much like Delacroix's *Greece*, in that it devised a way of presenting the events of Missolonghi with a view to affect the future of the Greek cause – both in pragmatic (the war effort) and discursive (the self-representation of Greeks) terms. It is, therefore, in this sense that *Nikiratos*'s patriotic rhetoric – or exposition of national ideologies and nationalist dreams – contributed to the making of the scenario of independence.

The Case of Theodoros Vryzakis

In his 1845 pamphlet titled *Where does the Art of the Greeks Tread Today*, philologist and archaeologist Stefanos Koumanoudis invited Greek artists to embrace European artistic trends as a means to re-discover their cultural roots – an argument reminiscent of Korais's project of *metakenosis*: 'in treating them [Europeans] as tutors in matters of art, much like the sciences, we do nothing else but moving toward the current owners of the ancient wisdom of our ancestors' (Koumanoudis, 1845: 7). Koumanoudis continues that, while the rest of Europe was in a process of transition from the Middle Ages to the Renaissance and, later, the Enlightenment, '[w]e Greeks [...] overwhelmed by the excess of foreign Asian ideas [...] remained sedated' (Koumanoudis, 1845: 10). Koumanoudis, following Korais, seeks to remedy this lack of a proper European education by turning to 'the current owners' of the nation's culture.

Educated in Philhellene King Ludwig's Munich under Friedrich Tiersch and influenced by Bavarian artists, Theodoros Vryzakis is a case in point in this cultural apprenticeship that Koumanoudis describes (cf. Koulouri, 2020: 66–77; Mertiri, 1993: 130–48; Kasimati, 2000). In his *Reception of Lord Byron at Missolonghi* (1861; see Figure 2) – an homage to Peter von Hess's *The Reception of Otto at Nafplion on 6 February 1833* (1852) – the 'classical closedness in the arrangement of the scene, the internal discipline, [...] the emphasis on anecdotal themes and the mise-en-scène of the exposition of the characters' produce a strikingly theatrical arrangement (Mertiri, 1993: 195): at the centre of the painting, Byron and his aide are presented standing next to Alexandros Mavrokordatos, a key political figure during and after the war. The rest of the painting is arranged in two concentric semi-circles: the inner one includes the local bishop and other militia leaders and local authorities, while the outer one is inhabited by the people of Missolonghi. Behind all these bodies, we see Missolonghi with a half-destroyed minaret rising above its skyline; further back, the gaze meets the mountains and the lagoon – geographical features that both specify and contain the scene. Finally, in the foreground of the painting, at the feet of Byron, the soil is being covered with olive branches – a sign of respect for the esteemed European guests.

The co-centric circles direct the viewer's gaze to the centre of the painting, at the space between Byron and Mavrokordatos. There, behind Byron, stands a woman who looks intensely at his direction. Her gaze determines the hierarchies dominating the relationship between the Greeks and the visitors. Most eyes, after all, are turned towards Byron, while the body language – particularly of those who are laying olive branches on the ground – shows great anticipation.

Figure 2 Vryzakis Theodoros (Thebes 1814 or 1819 – Munich 1878), *The Reception of Lord Byron at Missolonghi* (1861), Oil on canvas, 155 × 213 cm, Π.1298, © National Gallery – Alexandros Soutsos Museum, Photography Stavros Psiroukis

In addition, the way most Missolonghites are kneeling around him or hailing him with their arms raised toward the sky further accentuates such a hierarchy where they seek to be acknowledged by the gaze of the visitor. If in his *Exodus* he places the fighting Greeks in their desperate sacrifice centre-stage, here Vryzakis portrays the discovery of Greeks by the enlightened European Philhellene – the act upon which Greece's hopes rest.

The Greeks and foreigners are clearly distinguished by the way in which the two groups are dressed. Byron and his aide are dressed in European attire, while the people of Missolonghi and their leaders are dressed in what appears as a traditional Greek attire. The only exception is Mavrokordatos who also wears a black suit, which indicates another opposition at work during the war, that between native Greeks and the Greeks of the diaspora. In this context, the image of the three men in European attire standing out amidst a crowd of natives that look up to them reveals the European gaze of the artist as he produces a remarkably clear, yet idealised, illustration of the colonial hierarchies at work in the War of Independence: the native Greeks appear in the frame of visibility as an anonymous crowd, there only to reify the presence of Europeans and the Europeanised Greeks who actually make decisions. In addition, above his black suit, Byron is wearing a tunic: the 'current owner', to return to Koumanoudis's phrasing, of the classical tradition is there to enable the natives to (re)connect with their roots; at once paying tribute to the perceived descendants of the ancient Greeks and reminding them of the distance they have to cover in order to be recognised as such.

Finally, Byron's posture is reminiscent of a preaching Christ. Apart from implying that he arrives as a messiah, this reference also registers again and anew the binary opposition between Christianity and Islam. The presence of the local priest and the abundance of crosses surrounding the men at the centre of the painting further emphasise this: a strong use of Christian signifiers that is in stark opposition to the relative absence of Islam, whose only sign is the derelict minaret at the background. The evocation of this binary in a scene that does not include Ottomans rehearses the philhellenic argument, as per Christian solidarity: Greeks once again appear as suppliants to the Christian world.

Both *Byron's Reception* and the *Exodus* present the viewer with unambiguous ways of remembering the War of Independence. The idealised representation of Greeks as a collective – in both paintings, the Greeks are somewhat 'whitewashed' – and the centrality of the European gaze complement and illustrate the process of Hellenisation that was underway in the decades after the Greek state was formed. This process of Hellenisation that invents the Greeks as white against the arguments of conservative European circles lies at the basis of the scenario of independence; it memorialises embellished and idealised versions of events and people, reduces the complexity of history into simple narratives of suppliants and messiahs or heroes and villains and establishes the opposition between civilisation and barbarity in its many guises as the main drive behind the war – an opposition that dictates a historical determinism according to which modern Greece's destiny was to emerge as a white, Christian, liberal and European nation.

Delacroix's painting and Kairi's play were both products of their time and place in history: their primary political agenda was to call the European public to arms, not to memorialise the fall of Missolonghi for posterity. It is through the repetition of their discursive claims and performative repertoires that they are established and interpreted as constituents of the scenario of independence. Vryzakis's paintings, on the contrary, are examples of national efforts to construct a certain way of remembering the war and to repeat repertoires of independence that shaped modern Greek fictions of origin in the long, but not uncontested, process of Hellenisation. Integral to the scenario of independence, such repertoires stage the perceived continuities between the classical and the modern – where ancient Greeks in contemporary attire or modern

Greeks in ancient attire may dwell in and defend the contemporary city of Missolonghi. In addition, by rehearsing gestures of heroism and sacrifice, the scenario of independence firmly places the binary opposition between civilisation and barbarity and its twin opposition between Europeans and Ottomans at the basis of national imaginings, which in *Nikiratos* is further emphasised in the condemnation of Europeans that have 'defected' to the Other side. As such, the scenario places the living Greek subject in the position of the silent spectator and conjures in its stead the colonised ideal: the white European Hellene, who would gradually dominate, obscure and/or violently displace other communities and identities alongside their languages and dialects.[7] Thus, modern Greece was to become a monolingual and monocultural nation-state: a nation that, by virtue of performing the desire for national independence, mimics images of (neo)classical whiteness as a prerequisite for the emergence of the Greek nation-state, that is, mimics colonial desires and repressive practices to re-discover Greece as irrevocably European.

2 Independence and Revolution in Aris Biniaris's *'21*

In *'21*, Biniaris curated the national archive – written testimonies, declarations, announcements, proceedings from the revolutionary national assemblies, memoirs and other texts written and published between 1817 and 1835 – in a dramaturgy that was roughly structured in three sections: the uprising and the first battles; the siege and exodus of Missolonghi and the European responses to it; the creation of the Kingdom of Greece and the resistance of old independence fighters to the new order. In addition, while it was indeed a commemoration of the Greek War of Independence, Biniaris avoided any specific mention to actual names of people and places, thus turning the specific into a paradigmatic case. Rosi proposes that this iteration of the archive's fragments operates as 'a call to participate in a collective reassessment of fundamental notions [...] around freedom and revolution' (2021). If the Greek War of Independence becomes an exemplary case, its retelling is an invitation to consider what (fighting for) independence might be. Similarly,

---

[7] According to Roderick Beaton, the 'notorious Greek "language question" emerged in the mid-1760s' and concerned the language that 'future generations should be taught to write' and 'irrespective of whether they spoke Greek or a Slavic language or Vlach (Romanian), Albanian or even Turkish at home, it was this [...] written Greek language, along with their affiliation to the Orthodox Church, that brought them together' (2020: 24–5). Thus, the process of nationalisation gradually 'cleansed' the national body from other communities and their linguistic idioms. '[M]irror[ing] wider performances of Greek national identity', Greek theatre has a long history of monolingualism although there have been some attempts at multilingual performances in recent years (Fragkou, 2018: 301–6).

critic Annie Koltsidopoulou saw *'21* as a 'call for (individual or collective) revolution as a pursuit and a permanent philosophical question' (2015). In the following, I look at Biniaris's re-imagining of the scenario as a rehearsal of a revolutionary gesture in the context of the specific moment in the history of the Greek crisis in which it took to the stage of the Athens festival in the summer of 2015.

After months of intense negotiations between Greece's coalition government that was formed – by SYRIZA and Independent Greeks (a populist right wing party) – in January 2015 on an anti-austerity platform, the PM Alexis Tsipras called a referendum for 5 July 2015 that would decide whether Greece would accept the terms of a new deal proposed by its creditors. Should the electorate vote for it, this would be the third bailout package ostensibly seeking to resolve the country's fiscal insolvency. As such, the referendum came to stand for a vote for or against Europe: while the slogan of those campaigning for 'yes' was 'we stay in Europe', the opposing campaign focused on the word 'no' (*ohi* in Greek) and seemed to express a wider sense of resistance to the European Union. While the former exploited the fear of losing membership in the European Union, the latter played on the historical connotations of the word 'no' that, since World War II, has served as a statement of resistance to a foreign invader (cf. Hager, 2021). On the evening of 3 July 2015, Athens appeared as a divided city, as the two campaigns staged their final events only a few blocks from each other with the participation of politicians, celebrities and popular artists.[8] At the same time, a few kilometres away, Biniaris was enacting his take on the scenario of independence.

Crucial to his iteration of the scenario was the spatial arrangement of the performance area. Consisting of a large pyramid-shaped tent that occupied most of the stage, the set was, albeit on a much smaller scale, reminiscent of the pyramid stage of the Glastonbury Festival while also evoking military tents in wartime encampments (see Figure 3). Thus, the spatial arrangement supplied a performance site that facilitated the co-existence of multiple worlds that were, in turn, inhabited by the three performers who took on no other role than that of the musician/storyteller. Animations were projected at the back of the stage throughout the duration of the show, which further established connections with the imagery of rock concerts while also emphasising elements of the story that was being narrated. Rather than describing the scenes narrated or using visual signs specifically linked to the War of Independence, these projections loosely indicated actions and physicalities evoked in the

---

[8] Roughly a month later, and while the referendum results were overwhelmingly against the creditors' offer, the Greek government agreed to a different deal that continued the logic of crisis management without further challenge to the fiscal policies imposed by the EU and the IMF.

Figure 3 From left to right: Takis Varellas (Bass), Aris Biniaris (Guitar) and Vasilis Giaslakiotis (Drums) in '*21*. Photo Credit: Evi Fylaktou

Figure 4 From left to right: Takis Varellas (Bass), Aris Biniaris (Guitar) and Vasilis Giaslakiotis (Drums) in '*21*. Photo Credit: Evi Fylaktou

narration (see Figure 4). If the spatial arrangement evoked the war, therefore, it did so indirectly, as it mainly emphasised the act of storytelling and enabled the enactment of physical repertoires that were in line with the musical repertoires.

'21 was an unlikely staging of the archive of independence, as it did not rehearse any of the embodied, visual and musical repertoires that are customarily reproduced in theatrical or other commemorations of the war. Rosi points out that the play's (*'21*) 'most interesting aspect was the affective charge of the vocal performance' that was complemented by the use of music, whose composition, she continues, 'occurred as a response to the sound of the words' (2021). While it may be true that it was inspired by the texts, the music did not operate as a descriptive or complementary element. Rather, it guided the delivery of the text and punctuated meaning and the distribution of affects. Ileiana Dimadi writes that '[e]lectric blues for a shattered nation, psychedelic sambas for the hunger at Missolonghi and punk arias in support of the national struggle construct a rock oratorio' (Dimadi, 2015). The music served, in other words, as a way to listen, feel and interpret the scenes from the war invoked in the show; a medium for criticism, grief, sarcasm, irony and reflection – the means through which audiences would engage with the scenario of independence. Such an argument is further supported by the performers' embodied repertoires: a bass player whose body rocked to the sonic patterns his instrument was generating; a drummer sitting at his kit and his movement serving the sometimes gentle and other times erratic rhythms; a guitarist/singer who is sometimes approaching and other times moving away from the microphone that stood before him and sometimes playing his guitar but mostly letting it hang by his side. Three bodies that, much like in any rock concert, moved according to the instruments they were playing and the rhythms and textures of music they were producing. Three bodies unlearning the national repertoires by rehearsing the repertoires of the rock concert.

This backdrop provided for Biniaris a performative framework in which the staging of the war's archive could rewind national memory. This was further abetted by his decision to introduce and conclude the performance with extracts from the excommunication of the Greek uprising by the Patriarch of Constantinople Gregorios V and an earlier but similar text by the Patriarch of Jerusalem Anthimos titled *Fatherly Teachings*,[9] which called on Greeks to 'close their ears' to the 'contaminated' words of those advocating revolution: 'The devil, the mutinous devil [. . .] erected a new heresy, a novel scheme, the

---

[9] Patriarch Gregorios V presided over the synod that condemned the uprising on the basis that it was driven by ingratitude and rebelliousness against the head of the Ottoman Empire, the Sultan. He was executed by the Ottomans a few weeks later as he 'bore by virtue of his position the ultimate responsibility for the Greeks' loyalty' to the Ottoman Empire (Mazower, 2021: 33).

system of freedom'.[10] By bookending the dramaturgy with the official rejection of the insurrection by the Christian Orthodox church, Biniaris not only unsettled well-established mnemonic practices that present it as an active agent of resistance to the Ottomans but also framed the entire performance as a 'contaminated' and 'contaminating' song that lured the listener to the 'devil's path', the path of rebellion.

In this instance, Biniaris's playful delivery of the text provided a meaningful wordplay: the Greek word for song is *asma*, while the word for contamination is *miasma*. Biniaris's delivery of the phrase 'contaminating song' (*asma miasma*) separated the first syllable from the word miasma, thus making it *mi-asma*. Moreover, *mi-* is a negating prefix; thus, *mi-asma* also means non-song or an inappropriate song. In this sense, what followed was sought to be contaminating (and contaminated) not only because it rehearsed revolutionary arguments but also because it did so beyond 'accepted' mnemonic repertoires – outside the imperial field of visibility both in terms of the kind of songs/music that enable this retelling and the perspective from which the story is narrated. Coupled with his decision to stage his retelling of the war as a punk rock oratorio, this ironically delivered introduction and conclusion to the performance made Biniaris's punk song even more unsettling: the words of the two patriarchs rehearsed the binary opposition between civilisation and barbarity, but the terms were changed to god and devil. As such, the rebellious Greeks fighting for independence became barbaric subjects who chose the path of the devil, while the father figures – agents of order (god, the Sultan, the Bavarian first king of the independent Greek state and the Christian Orthodox Church) – became the representatives of civilisation. By unsettling the terms of the binary, therefore, *'21* revealed a much more complex web of allegiances, oppositions and loyalties than is implied in the binary driving the philhellenic gaze and, subsequently, the scenario of independence.

This was further articulated towards the end of the performance in the story of 'a young man of 25 years, an armatole since he was a child' who, upon King Otto's arrival, decided to leave for the mountains in a bid to resist the new father: when bidding farewell to his wife, he says, 'the present rulers are the offspring of conquerors; they seek to enslave us again'. The young armatole's monologue is an illustration of the words of iconoclastic author Yiannis Skaribas, whose book *1821 and the Truth* was Biniaris's starting point: '[f]ighting a revolution and overthrowing the tyrant is not much. This is what [18]21 did. Not to be enslaved again, this is the real revolution' (1995: 9). If *'21* was indeed an invitation to renegotiate notions of freedom and revolution, as per Rosi's suggestion, the young armatole served as a mouthpiece for it, while his

---

[10] All excerpts from the performance are from its run in the 2015 Athens Festival.

words served as a bridge between the past and the present. As in 2015 Greece's independence was threatened by yet another incarnation of Skaribas's tyrant in the shape of the debtocratic regime imposed by Greece's creditors, such a reminder that the War of Independence merely resulted in Greece's crypto-colonial status charted the historical lineage of Greece's current state of dependency: 'Remember, my heart. Remember a looted and fractured country where corrupt men are rampant [...]. Remember a people that without any help [...] attempted to break with their tyrant [...]. Remember me too'. The reference to a corrupt and powerful elite against a backdrop of a dispossessed yet determined people would have rung familiar to an audience who, after five years of severe austerity and suppression of dissenting voices, had disregarded the 'sensible' voices and voted for a left-wing government that had promised to renegotiate the terms of the bail out and, in a temporary act of defiance of the European 'fathers', had even asked for a popular vote on the terms of a new proposed deal (cf. Zaroulia and Hager, 2014).

In Biniaris's punk oratorio, therefore, the armatole's call resonated less as a commemoration of the historical struggle than, as Dimitris Tsatsoulis proposes, an exploration of 'the strength [implied in] individual, social, national emancipation from whatever oppresses them: from all sorts of tyrants, with struggles, arms and blood' (2015). In this iteration, therefore, the scenario of independence re-activated revolutionary politics as a process through which a community might start to remember and work towards emancipation by undoing national independence. Read in the context of the summer of 2015, the civilised father was re-incarnated in the neocolonial establishment and those supporting the continuation of the debtocratic regime. Their voices, *'21* seems to suggest, echo those voices condemning the 1821 uprising as the work of the devil; voices that see any deviation from the progress represented by European integration as barbaric and, by extension, condemn the 'system of freedom' as 'heresy'.

The central section of the performance that revolved around the siege of Missolonghi outlined the liminal position of independence fighters and, indeed, all revolutionary subjects – a position whose paradigmatic case was Missolonghi: they (as a collective) did not see the fruits of their struggle, but neither were they defeated. The account stops at the moment of the exodus, the liminal moment, when 'the enemy's bombs were falling incessantly' and the exiting horde cried:

'[Go] forward! [...] It's not a big deal'. Marshlands could not contain them, nor could forests. 'Forward! It's not a big deal'. [...] As they ran forwards, behind them the city [seemed] like a furnace. As they ran, they had already proven to the world that they were worthy of their freedom; they had already fought for their indefeasible rights. They had suffered a lot, they were deprived of many things, they had bathed in blood, they had wet their bread with tears

Their rebellious act is suspended in mid-air – never succeeding, never failing; much like in Vryzakis's painting, we keep seeing them in that moment, where even though they did not win the battle, they had won their independence. Contrary to Vryzakis's painting, however, this section offers nuance partly because of certain details that are based on the memoirs of general Nikolaos Kasomoulis – one of the leaders of the garrison who survived the exodus – that reveal the rough reality of the siege and partly due to the choices of music in this section.

It started in a fast paced 'psychedelic samba', a frantic passage that focused on the theme of hunger. Biniaris's narration recounted how the inhabitants of Missolonghi started eating horses, then donkeys, dogs, cats, frogs, rats and seaweed. 'There was no more food', he sang in a semi-sarcastic tone, 'day by day the hunger was increasing; [. . .] they slaughtered a horse; they ate it, they cooked it, they complimented the food; it was the most delicious food. In a few days there were no more horses'. The same 'stanza' was then repeated for the rest of the animals. In the end: 'what other choice did they have, but to drink blood'. The hunger section ended in a frenzied crescendo, while Biniaris was repeating the words 'curious mix'. The particular section, overlaid with sarcasm, conflated historical fact – the actual lack of food during the siege – with its narrativisation in Kasomoulis's memoirs and, finally, the impoverishment of the Greek population during the crisis that led many to soup kitchens. The besieged had, by this stage in the performance, been reduced to wild animals, eating whatever they could find; they were deprived of their humanity for the sake of being recognised by the European gaze. Indeed, a 'curious mix' – sarcasm was key here as it undid the fetishised and heroic narrativisation of the famine in Missolonghi to expose the irrational desperation of actual hunger – very differently endured and yet not so distant in 2015.

Wild animals as they had become, they decided to fight their way out of the city like 'raging and fuming tigers'. After the frantic atmosphere of the hunger section, the preparations for the exodus were detailed in grave silence. This section was signposted by acts of desperation, such as the decision to give opium to children to keep them quiet during the exodus; the farewells and the wish on the lips of the men refusing to wear clean clothes offered by the women, 'if only we get out'. This abrupt shift in the pace and texture of the narration emphasised the gravity of the situation, while Biniaris's delivery expanded the feral metaphor as he spoke the words in a low voice, almost concocting the image of a feline lurking in darkness, preparing to attack. Still wild animals, the besieged were no longer uncivilised but dignified; the irony was substituted with a grave sense of astonishment at the decision and the planning for the act of the exodus. As the exodus began, the music started again; it was a slow blues rhythm that gradually gained momentum as the narration progressed from the rain that washed everything away to the climax where 'fuming tigers' ran towards enemy lines. The cries to move 'forward' marked both the bravery and the desperation of the besieged. Yet, as independence fighters exited the besieged city, none of the evocations of Hellenic bravery that customarily follow the Missolonghites was present here – they were no longer the descendants or modern incarnations of Leonidas and his 300 (cf. Athanassoglou-Kallmyer, 1989: 41–65): they appeared before the European gaze as savages.

After the exodus, Biniaris continued, the European public discovered the ancient nation in the ruins of Missolonghi – not the wild animals; victims, not savages: 'Here, the virtuous kings, the magnates offer their condolences, their sympathies. The whole world has given pity. The dawn of a new hope soothes the pain of their sufferings'. His sarcastic delivery of the text comments on the European sympathy that arrived after the event to discover a worthy cause. 'What might be the award', asks Biniaris only to start describing the terms under which independence is gained:

> The new father brings a great amount of money. The new father brings guarantees of peace, of hope, of happiness for the healthy motherland. Embrace the new king with gratitude and love. Faithful subjects embrace his throne – it is the only reward that is asked of them. And those of you who dared taking up arms, submit them at once

The new king brings hope on the basis of submission to his order. The people shall be nationalised under the watchful gaze and guardianship of their benefactors, the new king and his European allies. It is against this order that the young armatole bids farewell to his wife and leaves for the mountains. He asks her to remember him: not as a Hellene but as a tiger; as a wild subject that refused to be nationalised – an eternal Other that dwells outside of the imperial field of visibility, that is, a permanently revolutionary subject.

Once the text ended, the archive concluded and the music faded away, and the drummer produced a lyre and played a final melancholic tune. Biniaris's staging of the scenario of independence, thus, came full circle: the revolutionary subject re-discovered and embraced its Balkan roots – the young armatole and his wife, the subjects of the (new) father's oppression, while remaining invisible before the national and the European colonial gaze, were consciously and decidedly untangled from the Hellenic ideal in order to unearth a revolutionary – that is anti-imperialist – history. Rosi suggests that Biniaris approached the 'historical archive as a stock of images and texts that need to be activated differently [. . .] to address the contemporary audience, which seeks to find points of reference in a parched, dead tradition that has lost its living connection with the present'

(2021). Biniaris's curation and performance of the archive managed, in other words, to stage the history of the War of Independence with renewed urgency, and, through the use of unlikely repertoires, it reclaimed the fundamental tenets of the mnemonic scenario with a view to unlearn the work of Hellenisation. In this sense, by staging the archive, Biniaris sought to stage a revolutionary repertoire. And this, perhaps, was the bridge between the past and the present, the main intervention of *'21*: against the neocolonial onslaught in the age of neoliberal capitalism, as it was exemplified in the handling of the Greek debt crisis by Europe's leadership, Biniaris's rock oratorio advocated a renewed proliferation of revolutionary politics as the starting point of a politics of de-colonisation.

3 Independence and (Post)Industrial Space in Eleni Efthymiou's Free Besieged

Writing about Dionysios Solomos (1798–857), the author of *Free Besieged*, Calotychos suggests that, '[a]ppropriately for the discourse of ab-sense, this Greek who spoke little Greek and had never visited the Greek state was to be universally accepted as the first National Poet of modern Greece' (2003: 81). Having lived in Zakynthos and Corfu, in 1849, Solomos received the Gold Cross of the Knights of the Saviour 'due to the Greek sentiments expressed in so many of [his] poems which aroused enthusiasm at the time of the struggle for our country in its independence' (Jenkins 1940: 179; quoted in Calotychos 2003: 74). Nevertheless, his nationalisation effectively began with the first edition of his unfinished works by Iakovos Polylas in 1859 under the title *Found Works*, in the preface of which the editor 'casts Solomos as the National and Romantic Poet' (Calotychos, 2003: 74). Then, in 1865, the first two stanzas of his lengthy *Hymn to Liberty*, inspired by the War of Independence, became the lyrics of the Greek National Anthem.

A 'key aspect of Solomos's principle of creation' is, according to Eratosthenis Kapsomenos, 'the continual recreation of the text in new variations and new clusters of thematic and expressive units which never manage to realize their final form' (1992; quoted in Calotychos, 2003: 80). Such a creative process was in line with German romanticism that, 'following Schlegel and Novalis, does not aspire to being, but is a process' (Calotychos, 2003: 80). Solomos's mature work only exists in drafts – in fragments that do not follow a linear or progressive development but reflect different phases in the poet's engagement with the themes he explores. One such text is *Free Besieged* that was written in three drafts between 1829 and 1844 and was inspired by Missolonghi's siege. Tziovas proposes that Solomos 'did not aim at representing history or communicating reality, but through a process of poetic distillation and aesthetic abstraction, at capturing [its] essence' (1999: 178). Solomos's narrative, therefore, is not invested with any semblance of historical accuracy; it expresses a search for an ideal that never fully materialises. Rather than outlining its crystallised form, hence, the three drafts of *Free Besieged* seem to sketch out an ever-elusive nation; a 'utopian homeland', as per Vassiliki Dimoula's proposition, that 'is evoked as the "Other" that cannot be contained within the work', in which it is ultimately 'registered [. . .] through the impossibility of ever being named' (Dimoula, 2018: 207). It is, thus, this impossibility as well as the fragmentariness and unfinished character of the work that outlines Solomos's utopian political project.

The Romantic Poet Solomos seems at odds with the scenario of independence – his homeland is a work in progress: a search for an ideal rather than an idealised nation. Yet, Solomos, as the National Poet, emerges as an agent of national ideology and his work is transformed into a historical document that participates in a wider national topography. His nationalisation that, as mentioned earlier, begins with Polylas, who places him within the context of an 'aesthetic nationalism', was completed by his canonisation by another national poet, Kostis Palamas, who approached fragmentariness as an aesthetic aspect of Solomos's work (Dimoula, 2018: 202–3). Solomos's oeuvre has become, thus, part of the national canon and, as such, is confined in the scenario of independence and, rather than an unfinished utopian project, rehearses a concrete and crystallised image of the nation.

Efthymiou presented her rendition of *Free Besieged* in June 2021 as part of the Eleusis 2023 European Cultural Capital's celebratory programme for the bicentenary and was under direct commission from its artistic director Michael Marmarinos.[11] The production took place in the parking lot of Elefsina's defunct oil mill – part of the landscape of one of the industrial zones in the vicinity of Athens. Heaps of soil were scattered in the performance area among and on top of which the performers (see Figure 5), a 'diverse crowd' composed of fifty residents of Elefsina and neighbouring areas and five professional actors, re-enacted the siege of Missolonghi (Eleusis 2023, 2021b). There were also three musicians performing within that space, while members from the Municipal Philharmonic Orchestra of Elefsina stood in for the invaders and appeared on stage on a small truck and a crane. Performers, either in unison or individually, delivered the text, while sometimes they would explain or

---

[11] All events that form the programme of Eleusis 2023 are presented as 'Mysteries', an homage to the Elefsinian Mysteries – religious rituals held in ancient Elefsina in honour of goddess Demeter and her daughter Persephone. The actual title of the performance as presented in the programme was *Mystery 39: 'The Free Besieged'*.

Figure 5 *Mystery 39: 'The Free Besieged'*. Photo Credit: Angelos
Christophilopoulos

contextualise the text and other times they would share thoughts and/or stories
on freedom. The aim was, as per Efthymiou's admission, for Solomos's text to
'echo [. . .] in a narration concerning the recent past, but also the here and now;
a relentless present and a future that hovers above us like an inverted question
mark' (Eleusis 2023, 2021b). *Free Besieged*, therefore, served as the ground
upon which the performers would construct a temporality that enables
a 'conversation between the past and the present, the reinterpretation of the
historical events that marked the course of the modern Greek state, the relationship between those Besieged and their present counterparts in a modern city
with a long history' (Eleusis 2023, 2021b); a temporality reminiscent of Walter
Benjamin's conceptualisation of 'now-time [*Jetztzeit*]' as time 'blast[ing]
open the continuum of history' (Benjamin, 2003: 396). Solomos's
Missolonghites and Elefsina's residents, thus, meet to think together what
independence might mean in an uncertain future or how they might shape their
future together, in independence.

   Dressed in simple everyday clothes in shades of beige and brown, the
besieged entered the performance area, in a long line, a procession of sorts
that, among other things, enacted industrial repertoires – it brought to mind
images of industrial workers waiting in line to enter their workplace – and the
repertoire of the exodus – the procession. This ambivalence continued throughout the performance as they dispersed: the performers' physicality as they

moved and worked in space consistently evoked Solomos's Missolonghi while also conjuring industrial repertoires – something that was abetted by the cityscape/scenery and its soundscapes. In this formulation, the besieger deliberately remained – or was made – ambiguous: as per Efthymiou's directorial note, it can be 'whatever confines and deprives [the besieged] of life and dignity' (Eleusis 2023, 2021b).

In order to further pursue this argument, a brief consideration of the context in which the performance occurred is in order. The bid for Eleusis 2023 European Cultural Capital focuses on the notion of transition as a central theme and proposed outcome of its programme: '[t]ransition', it is suggested, 'is inscribed in the foundational myth of the city, in the tale of Persephone', while the city's past comprises 'a history of consecutive transitions' (Eleusis 2023, 2021a: 3–4). This history of transitions is closely linked to Elefsina's industrial development, which occurred in three main waves: the first between 1875 and 1906, the second between 1923 and 1939, and the third between 1948 and 1971. As Nikos Belavilas, Tatiana Saiti and Kalliopi Psarioti observe, industrialisation – particularly the installation of steelworks, shipyard and petrochemical units in the 1960s – had a huge environmental impact due to pollution as well as the 'privileged position [of industrial units] on the seafront that blocked the plain and residential zones from the sea' (2011: 5). In the latter quarter of the twentieth century, Greece went through a process of de-industrialisation, which, however, has not affected Elefsina as much as other former industrial zones, as industrial activity in the wider area endured and expanded with new kinds of activities. Nevertheless, most inner-city industrial units have closed and their now abandoned or even derelict buildings largely define the urban fabric (cf. Belavilas et al., 2011; Katsikis and Tsagkarakis, 2010).

Responding to the partial de-industrialisation of the inner-city, a new developmental model emerged in the beginning of the twenty-first century, with the establishment of the festival of Aeschylea and other initiatives that focus on cultural production (Eleusis 2023, 2021a: 2–3). The bid for Eleusis 2023 expands this framework and, while aspiring to dissociate Elefsina from the stereotypical image of an industrial city, seeks to showcase the (living) industrial memories through a 'renewed understanding of public art' that 'rests on the interaction between artists and non-conventional cultural sites, such as the old Oil-mill [. . .], as well as the people and the city's profile' (Eleusis 2023, 2021a: 23). The ambition of Eleusis 2023, therefore, is to engage closely with the industrial history and the communities that have experienced its consequences as well as the impact of its partial de-industrialisation in order to substitute industrial with cultural economies. Eleusis's ambition is, in other words, to facilitate a transition from industrial production to the production of post-industrial spaces.

In *Street Theatre and the Production of Postindustrial Space: Working Memory*, David Calder argues that street theatres – which, following Sylvie Clidière's definition, are theatres that 'need only occur outside of purpose-built performance spaces' (Calder, 2018: 8) – facilitate new uses of defunct industrial sites both in terms of the material reconfiguration of those sites and the discursive practices that institute them. As former industrial sites, he proposes, are transformed into cultural spaces where repertoires from the industrial past are enacted but not represented, the connections between past and present are established. The performers, themselves workers of the culture industry, are not called to embody the displaced industrial workers; they 'are not historical re-enactors [. . .]. Neither are they surrogates' (Calder, 2018: 182). Rather, in occupying post-industrial sites, they 'embody the accumulation of labour, the simultaneous persistence and transformation of repertoires, the emergence of the ostensibly or actually new from the recombination of extant behaviours and tropes' (Calder 2018: 182). They evoke, in other words, industrial repertoires while instituting new ones in the context of the transition to post-industrial economies and spaces.

In such an analytical framework, the defunct oil mill that is temporarily occupied by performers in Efthymiou's *Free Besieged* and more permanently used by cultural organisations since the early 2000s decoded Solomos's text: as the oil mill still carries the traces of its former use, the 're- or dis-placed' industrial workers, as Calder would have it, are 'still here' (2018: 182). This was true not only in a hauntological sense but also in corporeal terms: some of the residents participating in the production had been and still were industrial workers in the area. The presence of the building, now dilapidated, at the backdrop commands meaning-making mechanisms, although it was also temporarily transformed by projections of live-feed from the stage action; projections that 'documented' the minutiae of the labour of the cultural workers now operating in the building. In addition, the configuration of the performance space with heaps of soil and the use of the car and the crane enhanced the enactment of industrial repertoires by evoking its imagery and soundscapes. In other words, even though the narrative of the performance did not engage directly with Elefsina's industrial history, its *mise-en-scène* relied on its signs. As such, while the performers narrated the history of the siege of Missolonghi, their embodied repertoires and the overall scenic, visual and aural dramaturgy enacted the story of the industrial and post-industrial transitions of Elefsina. The re-territorialisation of Solomos's text was, therefore, accomplished by its incorporation in a new (urban) context that carried its own history and its own besiegers.

Scene 5, 'The besieger's desire to conquer Missolonghi', began with a banging on a thunder sheet – its sharp, menacing sound introducing the besieger.[12] One of the performers announced that 'the leader of the enemy forces, the *besieger*, delays his once hurried pace. [...] *The besieger. He who sees our city as a trophy. He who enters our nightmares. He who sees us as (movement of money)'*. Subsequently, and using Solomos's words, he proceeded to speak as the besieger of the land that he has failed to conquer – revealing his sorrow and shame over this failure. At this, the performer commented: 'Do you really feel shame besieger?' As the scene unfolds, other voices described the emotional impact of the imminent fall of Missolonghi in the neighbouring Ionian Islands and the sailors in the passing ships:

The islands around are afraid, they plead and cry
Even the foreign quartermasters feel sour from afar

The generalised sorrow on the side of the defenders turned to anger when the Europeans' failure to help is mentioned. As the anger of the onlookers grew, so did the besieger's frustration. The scene ended with him shouting, frustrated: 'Do you know who I am?' Then bells rang and the besieged stood still.

The besieger was at once the Ottoman leader and the industrialist. The city's ruins were for him a profitable or profiteering arena. The commentary on Solomos's text, which was derived from the words uttered and the bodies that uttered them – performers that embodied the Missolonghites but who were also residents of Elefsina defending their city against the profiteering of industrial capital – de-stabilised the narrative. Moreover, the dilapidated building of the oil mill stood in for the ruins of Missolonghi as well as being itself a remnant of Elefsina's industrial history. The two temporalities collapsed, therefore, upon the theatrical space to construct the temporality of history; a 'now-time' that invested the bodies of performers with the accumulation of the besieger's violence; with the simultaneous persistence and transformation of the repertoires of imperial violence: war, exploitation, profiteering, displacement, environmental catastrophe, unemployment and destitution.

Against this besieger, Efthymiou's production seemed to propose solidarity as the way towards an emancipated and sustainable future. In the director's note, she asks, 'what might we have to lose for the words "together" and "solidarity" to be interwoven with our breathing?' (Eleusis 2023, 2021b). In light of the history of Missolonghi, the phrasing of this question seems apt: the reference to loss as the necessary process through which a community might come together and develop

---

[12] All excerpts from the performance are taken from an unpublished version of the text that was kindly provided by the director.

ties of solidarity is relevant to the history of Missolonghi – a city that lost everything but its ties of solidarity – as much as it is pertinent in the history of Elefsina – a city that is in danger of losing everything unless it develops such ties. One might also add that solidarity as an answer to the violence of the besieger is apposite in the wider context of the ongoing Greek crisis or rather that, since the beginning of the debt crisis, it has been initiatives and gestures of solidarity that enabled Greeks to endure neoliberal barbarity – initiatives that included soup kitchens, social surgeries and the 'potato movement', which saw farmers selling their produce directly to the consumers and local markets using alternative currencies. Togetherness and solidarity, therefore, comprised the meeting ground for past and present; a platform for Efthymiou's meeting with Solomos's text, the residents of Elefsina and the audience.

The repertoires of solidarity as pre-conditions for freedom were explored more closely in Scene 3, 'The Flag': some men from the 'crowd' ran to a large heap of soil at the far end of the performance area and started to dig, while the rest of the company got back in a line. The 'diggers' found a thick rope that was gradually passed on to everyone in the line – the movement of the rope was captured by a camera and projected onto the wall of the oil mill (see Figure 6). This instance also marked the only major deviation from Solomos's text as, while the rope was passed on, members of the chorus of the besieged shared their thoughts on solidarity and freedom. There were three main contributions. The first one told

Figure 6 *Mystery 39: 'The Free Besieged'.* Photo Credit: Angelos Christophilopoulos

a parable about sharing and solidarity as a basis for happiness. The second offered short statements on the meaning of freedom, relating to everyday or personal acts of defiance, such as '[f]reedom is [. . .] shouting against the majority. Telling the truth. Saying "I love you". Coming out to your friends. Becoming the neighbour-hood's Don Quixote. [. . .] Coming to terms with death'. The third contribution is the one that I will discuss in more detail. Starting with a story of togetherness and comradeship from his childhood, which, for him, is evoked when he thinks of freedom, a man went on to propose that to be 'free but alone is meaningless'. Freedom here relies on solidarity and togetherness and, as such, 'to fight for the right to freedom is the greatest revolution of our times'.

Such an understanding of freedom evoked Hannah Arendt's discussion of freedom as a political question, rather than a philosophical one. Freedom, she argues, cannot be understood as something that exists outside of collective human action and draws a comparison between the realm of politics and the performing arts:

> Performing artists –dancers, play-actors, musicians, and the like– need an audience to show their virtuosity, just as acting men need the presence of others before whom they can appear; both need a publicly organised space for their 'work', and both depend upon others for the performance itself. [. . .] If then we understand the political in the sense of the polis, its end or *raison d'être* would be to establish and keep in existence a space where freedom as virtuosity can appear (Arendt, 2006: 152–3)

The notion of virtuosity, the space of appearance that comprises the arena of the political, and the notion of work that ties everything together propose a conceptualisation of freedom as a performative gesture, as opposed to freedom as an institution; freedom as an embodied repertoire that requires work and commitment alongside and before – or in solidarity with – others to achieve and be recognised as virtuosic.

In light of this, this scene and the particular contribution seemed to produce a space of appearance, which was also a theatrical space, where the repertoires of solidarity were acted out in a state of becoming, unfinished, resting on action. By the same token, freedom could be rehearsed only as long as the community of the besieged passed on the rope; only for as long as they dug and pulled together. This is where they met Solomos's utopian homeland, which appeared in the spaces between the bodies of the performers-citizens; in the spaces of solidarity. Thus, the community rehearsed onstage undid the national register, even in its utopian iteration: the performers were all residents of Elefsina, but some were also migrants, either internal or external – a 'diverse crowd' that was not connected on the basis of national lineage or a shared history but of conviviality. To further emphasise this point, the expert finished his contribution by denouncing borders as divisive mechanisms that hinder performances of freedom, somewhat reminiscent of Azoulay's contention that progress as an instrument of imperial history aims at destroying the earth as a shared space: 'We all stand on the same earth, breathe the same air, look at the same sky'.[13] The clash with the besieger can only be realised so long as 'we' stand together and are willing to lose disjunctive configurations: 'Freedom and death, not freedom or death. This disjunctive "or" only knows division', the man says in the end.

The word revolution, loaded in many different ways, particularly in the context of the Greek Revolution, is the signal for the besiegers to break out into singing: 'And the sky was revelling, the earth was applauding/Every moving voice toward the light it was speaking'. The revolutionary axiom of 1821 slipped as national repertoires of independence were rewound. The sky was revelling indeed and the earth was applauding a formation, even if only imaginary, whereby the people uttering these words were no longer Missolonghites or the people of Elefsina but a community erecting its together-ness in solidarity against the violence of any besieger that may come its way. Its revolution is not spelt with a capital 'R', as it is not the work of heroes but that of everyday people whose bodies were not only tied together in the act of pulling the rope but also quite literally tied together by the rope. At the end of the rope, they unearthed a large flag resembling the Greek revolutionary flag that, instead of a white cross against a blue backdrop, was a soiled beige cloth with a brown cross.

Just before the end, the besieged got into battle positions. They picked up stones from the ground and threw them towards the enemy lines. They resem-bled street fighters, battling the forces of the (nation-)state – yet another incarnation of the besieger. Then, they formed the line once again, this time to stage their exodus. Singing with their fists up in the air, they left the space, rehearsing the embodied repertoire of the exodus. While their image was projected onto the wall of the oil mill, an elderly man stayed behind. He recited the first stanza of the third draft of the *Free Besieged*, an invocation of the homeland as the 'magnanimous mother', a 'goddess' whose voice the poet cannot hear. The man left the microphone and walked towards the dilapidated building. This final scene, instead of blasting the besieged city, blasted the historical continuum. The repertoires of the defenders of Missolonghi and the residents of Elefsina were once again transformed; this time into protesters from

---

[13] Azoulay argues that imperial history moves towards an endless destruction of a 'shared world – what people can and should care for together' (2019: 18).

the last decade that fought another besieger: the violence of neoliberalism that has shaken Greek society and has, once again, questioned its independence. The repertoire of the exodus – a procession, queue and demonstration – was in flux; as the bodies moved, dispersed and re-formed, they seemed to be 'keeping and transforming', to use Taylor's terms, 'choreographies of meaning' (2003: 20). As they all blended in the work of solidarity that materialised only for as long as the rope was being passed on and the fists were raised, they formed Solomos's utopian homeland, an unfinished and incongruous community – an elusive 'we'.

The scenario of independence re-surfaced in many instances: *Free Besieged*, in the context of national poetry, is a text that, regardless of what it might propose in its own right, has been colonised by the mere fact that its author has been cast as the National Poet; the embodied repertoires of the exodus as they were enacted in the line of bodies; the image of the flag that conjured the specific national history; and, finally, the binary opposition between civilisation and barbarity. Nevertheless, by virtue of being reiterated in the specific site, in the specific historical moment and by the specific diverse crowd, the constituent elements of the scenario were radically decoded, re-contextualised and adapted. Efthymiou's *Free Besieged* re-imagined the scenario of independence in the post-industrial transition and, in doing so, the negotiation of independence was altered because the national cause does not seem to apply any longer as the drive for a 'revolution'. Put differently, the particular production sought to unlearn the national revolution, as today's world requires a claim to independence that revolves around solidarity in the face of environmental catastrophe that is particularly visible in Elefsina as a result of its industrial development, the rising unemployment that is a consequence of de-industrialisation and the ongoing Greek crises and the xenophobic violence that seemed to drive the electoral rise of Golden Dawn and the wider legitimation of reactionary rhetoric and practices. It is in this framework that the archive was troubled: the flag, for example, did not evoke the clear purity of classical whiteness but was a dirty cloth. By the same token, Solomos was no longer the National Poet but his romantic alter ego. And the repertoires of the exodus seemed to establish themselves as the manifestation of solidarity and resistance against every besieger, not the enemies of the nation.

The civilisation–barbarity opposition, therefore, was reframed to consider current conditions of living in 'the city of Aeschylus, of history and of the ancient ruins, of industry, of civilisation and the barbarous environmental catastrophe, the contemporary city, a place shared by people from all over Greece and the world' (Eleusis 2023, 2021b). As they rehearsed repertoires of independence, the besieged – the agents of civilisation – were the defenders of Missolonghi as much as they were the producers of the post-industrial transformation of Elefsina and objects of neoliberal exploitation and extraction-ism. Similarly, the besieger – the agent of barbarity – summoned a shifting image of an aggressor whose only constant was the exercise of violence. In this iteration of the binary, therefore, the civilised 'we' evoked was not nationalised (or at least it had slipped from its crystallised nationalisation in the scenario of independence) but expansive; the barbarous enemy was far from fixed on its national, religious or racialised understanding – it was no longer the domain of the Non-European Other. Rather, it seemed to emerge as an opposition between the open-endedness of solidarity and the fixity of imperial violence. Therefore, this iteration of the scenario of independence prefigured a different kind of politics by unlearning imperial notions and experiences of independence. In this sense, the exodus is no longer a final sacrifice but a performative and militant gesture towards a de-colonised and sustainable future.

4 Independence and the Mythopoetics of the Stranger in Anestis Azas's the Republic of Baklava

Azas's *The Republic of Baklava* was part of 'Cycle 1821' at the 2021 Athens Festival – a section of the festival that celebrated the bicentennial of the War of Independence. Azas opened the performance by introducing the four perform-ers (Katerina Mavrogeorgi, Cem Yigit Üzümoglu, George Julio Katsis and Gary Solomon) who would present the results of the company's research on the story of Fatih and Sophia – 'a Greek-Turkish couple who tried to establish its own state starting from their baklava pastry-workshop in Missolonghi'.[14] After Fatih, Sophia and their son Meze settled in Missolonghi, everything seemed to be going well until little Meze was bullied in school.[15] This incident led Fatih and Sophia to make the decision to create an independent state, the Republic of Baklava.[16] The new state that was founded on a little island in the lagoon of Missolonghi initially attracted people from Western Europe and was treated as a harmless, even if somewhat scandalous, curiosity. This all changed once the first boat with refugees arrived in the Republic of Baklava: under pressure from its European allies, the Greek police and military forces laid siege and eventu-ally occupied the little island. During the final battle between the Greek forces and the Baklavanians, Fatih, Sophia and most of the island's citizens lost their lives. Little Meze was one of the few survivors.

---

[14] All excerpts are from the recording of the performance during its run in the 2021 Athens Festival that the director kindly shared with me. All non-English excerpts are cited in English as per the recording's subtitles.

[15] Meze in Greek and Turkish means appetiser.

[16] Baklava is a dessert claimed by different regions in the Middle East and South Mediterranean – such as Greece, Turkey, Jordan, Lebanon and Syria.

If in *'21* and *Free Besieged* the facticity of the real was evoked by the use of the actual archives of the War of Independence and the presence of 'real' people, respectively, in *The Republic of Balkava*, it emerged as a framing device: even though it was increasingly apparent that the story was indeed fictional, the performance employed recognisable documentary theatre tropes. The performers, introduced as 'a group of "researchers"' (ΕλCulture, 2022), presented 'documents' from their fieldwork: TV interviews, Sophia's personal diary, news broadcasts, readings of newspaper articles, social media posts, letters and emails, zoom recordings, recordings of phone conversations and records of the Republic of Baklava's assembly. Designed by Eleni Stroulia, the set supported the framing of the performance as a documentary as there was no attempt to create a 'realistic' space (see Figure 7); rather, Stroulia provided an almost empty space that contained a handful of objects that would enable the performers to tell that story: a few chairs, two fridges, three small tables, a tall trolley for trays, scattered bricks, a projection screen and a fixed structure made of neon lights hanging at the back of the stage. Apart from these, the performers used a synthesizer, a guitar and three microphones on their stands.

Nevertheless, very little evidence was actually presented in its materiality; rather, the four performers acted out the various 'documents'. In this sense, the performers operated as researchers/narrators and the story's protagonists or

Figure 7 From left to right: Cem Yigit Üzümoglu, Katerina Mavrogeorgi, George Julio Katsis and Gary Solomon in *The Republic of Baklava*. Photo Credit: Pinelopi Gerasimou

witnesses. In addition, the projection screen that, in documentary theatres, usually works as a medium for the presentation of evidence showed the same still image of the lagoon of Missolonghi for the duration of the show. Considering that the image of the lagoon was real as opposed to the fabricated evidence re-enacted in front of it, such a choice questioned the promise of the documentary while also inviting the audience to make connections between the (telling of the) fictional story and the (commemoration of the) history of Missolonghi; connections that were already implied in the programming of *The Republic of Baklava* as part of a section of the 2021 Athens Festival commemorating the bicentenary of the War of Independence. The pseudo-documentary form, therefore, worked to undo the authority of the document as a privileged site of authenticity, particularly in relation to historical re-enactment: rather than recounting the history of the siege of Missolonghi, Azas and the company presented a contemporary fable that revolved around another – fictional – siege that, according to critic Tonia Karaoglou, sought to engender an '"insolent" view on national(ist) myths, but also satire on the [operation of] the media and criticism on the handling of the matter of the refugees' (2022).

In light of the above discussion, the performance sought to expose 'stereo-types and prejudices that govern Greek society, as inextricable elements of a tradition of intolerance' (Mparas, 2022). Such a 'tradition of intolerance', which reflects on Greek as well as wider European Union border control policies, has become apparent in recent years as refugees trying to enter the EU, should they survive perilous sea crossings, become victims of state-sanctioned or spontaneous xenophobic violence, get 'stuck' in camps on the Greek islands under inhumane conditions or are pushed back to Turkey, while also encountering a hostile legal framework (cf. Cox and Zaroulia, 2016). An emblematic case in this respect was the 2014 shipwreck off the small east Aegean island Farmakonisi where eleven out of twenty-seven passengers drowned in what was, as per the ruling of the European Court of Human Rights, an attempt of the Greek coast guard to push the boat into Turkish waters (European Court of Human Rights, 2022). Azas's *Case Farmakonisi or The Right of Water* (2015) was a piece of documentary theatre that explored the shipwreck with a view to develop and document a counter-narrative to the official account of the events that acquitted the coast guard of any responsibility and charged one of the survivors as the 'trafficker'.

The argument I wish to pursue here is that *The Republic of Baklava* sought to demonstrate that the tradition of intolerance at work in such practices is manifest in national(ist) mnemonic repertoires – particularly of the War of Independence whose commemoration perpetually produces the binary

opposition of civilisation vs. barbarism again and anew. Moreover, in address-
ing this tradition of intolerance and exposing contemporary racist and xenophobic discourses, Azas and the company denationalised the discussion of
independence by way of re-imagining encounters with foreignness and undoing
what I call the mythopoetics of the stranger; that is, the consistent mythologisation of foreignness that enables the mis-recognition of strangers as such and,
subsequently, shapes strange encounters.

   In *Theatre & Migration*, Emma Cox stresses that, while migrant bodies are
politicised by the specific economic and political circumstances of their
border crossings, their recognition is dependent on what she calls 'a mythopoetics of migration' that is 'an accumulation of visions of foreignness that
have collided in the globalised, bureaucratised present' (2014: 10). This
notion of a mythopoetics, a 'making-myth' of migration, interests me here
as a process of classification and signification of bodies, which, by and large,
rests upon the assumption that migrant bodies exist 'out of their time', as per
Cox's phrasing, by way of participating in a long history of migrant itineraries,
which overwrites the specificities of their conditions of migration (2014: 11).
I am, therefore, borrowing the notion of mythopoetics from Cox to signify this
marking of bodies as strange; as bodies that seem to appear out of their time,
even if their being strangers is a result of their specific economic and political
circumstances.

   In *Strange Encounters: Embodied Others in Post-Coloniality*, Sara Ahmed
maintains that the act of recognition of strangers involves a knowing again:
'[r]ecognising strangers [. . .] is a question of how to survive the proximity of
strangers who are already figurable, *who have already taken shape*, in the
everyday encounters we have with others' (2000: 22). The stranger is, in this
sense, not the one who cannot be recognised; rather, it is the one who is already
recognisable as being out of place. Considering this, recognition of the stranger
delineates the borders of one's space of safety – one's 'home' and 'proper' ways
of moving in it; it produces strange bodies 'as impossible and phobic object[s]'
while also 'establish[ing] the domain of the privileged subject (his bodily
world)' (Ahmed, 2000: 54). The appearance of the stranger, therefore, sets in
motion and exposes an 'economy of xenophobia' (Ahmed, 2000: 54) that acts
on mythologies of strange bodies that 'threaten to traverse the border that
establishes the "clean body" of the white subject' (Ahmed, 2000: 52).
Recognition of the stranger as such, in other words, contributes to and is fed
by the mythopoetics of the stranger.

   In light of this, I wish to focus on two instances from *The Republic of Baklava*
that are central to the unfolding of the dramaturgy and its undoing of the
mythopoetics of the stranger: the first one is the incident involving Meze's

abuse by his classmates at school during rehearsals for a patriotic play re-enacting the War of Independence – titled *Nikitaras the Turk-Eater* – where Meze was instructed to play the 'Turk'. The second is the impact of the arrival of a refugee, Bashat, which marked a moment after which 'nothing was the same any longer'.

Meze's bullying was staged by presenting the documents of its aftermath: the initial emails exchanged between his parents expressing their concern and 'demand[ing] the removal and exemplary punishment of Mr Lichnarakis', the school's teachers detailing the events and the parents' association that responded that 'you named your child Meze, you should have expected that the other children would want to eat him'; Mr Lichnarakis's apology where he argued that he was unaware that Meze was hurt; the nation-wide controversy it sparked in the media where theatre critics debated whether such violence was indeed artistic expression or a blatant case of xenophobic bullying, all the while breeding anti-Turkish propaganda; protests in the Greek capital against bullying, counter-protests against anti-national(ist) propaganda;, finally, the attack on Fatih and Sophia's shop and workshop in Missolonghi by nationalists, who left behind 'flyers with nationalist slogans and ate the whole store'. Some of these flyers – documents attesting to the veracity of the narration – were brought onstage and read out loud before being thrown onto the audience: 'you will never become Greek little Meze'.

Meze's casting as the 'Turk' – the national enemy – and the subsequent acts of violence exposed and re-activated a mechanism of recognition of foreign-ness; foreignness that, up to that point, was mis-recognised for acceptance – Fatih was accepted by Missolonghites *even though* he was a Turk. In an earlier scene that anticipated Meze's bullying, this mis-recognition was further nuanced: in a Greek issue of *Classics Illustrated* about independence fighter and national martyr Athanasios Diakos (cf. Sampatakakis, 2021b: 283–6), the Greeks were shown fighting the Ottomans who were represented, as per Fatih's description, as 'blackface Arabs' (see Figure 8). Subsequently, Fatih confused the Greeks for Ottomans, and after Sophia explained, he replied, 'So they blackface the Turks?' While Fatih and Sophia were having this discussion in English, the other two performers held a giant copy of the comic book and read out in Greek the dialogue between Diakos and the Ottoman leader where the life of a 'Turk' is described by the Greek fighter as 'infidel and ignoble'. By mistaking the 'infidels' for Greeks and thus failing to recognise his 'kin', Fatih misplaced himself as a member of the community in Missolonghi, whereas, in actuality, he was the 'blackfaced Turk' as far as the local community was concerned – a phobic object that threatened the body of the nation. In addition, if, by rehearsing the scenario of independence, the point of the comic

Figure 8 From left to right: Gary Solomon and George Julio Katsis in *The Republic of Baklava*. Photo Credit: Pinelopi Gerasimou

book was to recognise Ottomans as dark-skinned barbarians leading uncivilised lives, Üzümoglu's presence as an actual Turk whose appearance did not conform to the representation of the Turk in the comic book seemed to reverse the borders, as set out by the scenario of independence, between the European self and the Orient's barbarity.

Foreignness was further recognised in a nightmare Sophia had following the bullying incident: this dream, as read out from Sophia's diary, interspersed the violence of national commemorations of the war with her family's experience of xenophobic violence and 'reminded her why she left in the first place'.[17] The dream's climax was a parade featuring 'the hundreds of thousands non-combatant dead of [the revolution of] 1821, Christians and Muslims' and 'all that looked like the 2004 Olympics opening ceremony'. Finally, a priest who had earlier in the dream examined Fatih's knowledge of national history and now was discovered to be Papaflessas – a hero of the War of Independence – approached

---

[17] Before the nightmare, the actual history of the War of Independence had been evoked either directly in the comic book scene and the play staged at Meze's school or indirectly when, during a TV interview Fatih and Sophia gave to a local channel in Missolonghi, advertisements for fictional Lord Byron themed products – anti-mosquito lotion, hay-fever tablets, dehumidifiers, etc. – were staged. These featured a dying Lord Byron performed in an exaggerated manner by Üzümoglu, whose attire was faintly reminiscent of Vryzakis's Byron, uttering Paul Valery's maxim 'we should not take things as tragic as they are'. These instances pointed at the kitsch aesthetic of parts of Greek popular culture and the kitsch, even farcical, representation of the national past.

her and whispered 'Sophia let little Jesus come inside you. Only this way you can partake in our nation, in our god, in our ancient civilization'. The dream was a culmination of Sophia's exposure to national(ist) mnemonic practices and the prejudices they reiterate; a culmination of what started as a farce and, after the bullying incident and its permutations across Greek society, climaxed as a nightmare.

The reference to the 2004 Olympics added another layer of national(ist) discourse. The procession at the centre of the opening ceremony narrated the history of Greeks from ancient times to the present day. It was, as per Plantzos's phrasing, an 'archaeological performance [. . .] whose images, while addressed to the international community, were in actuality characterised by introversion. They were inscribed on the national body [. . .] with a view to provide to collective imagination an appropriate spectacle for revival and admiration' (2016: 20–4). The procession, in other words, was a performance of colonial mimicry in the sense that it performed the Greek nation by way of rehearsing its self-colonisation. In this sense, the celebratory procession of the victims of the War of Independence in Sophia's nightmare seemed to suggest that the celebration of such barbarity is at the centre of national memory and its European identification. If the 2004 ceremony used the colonised image of the classical past to declare that the Greeks are (still) European, the procession in the dream used the usually invisible dead bodies of the Greek revolution to reaffirm this Europeanness. The nightmare, finally, marked the recognition by Sophia that, fuelled by the mythopoetics of the stranger, the violence exercised in the commemoration of the national past enabled the national body to re-form itself around its encounter with her family and predicted the fate of the Republic of Baklava as Europe's pariah.

Created at the back of the dream, the Republic of Baklava appeared initially as a 'land of the stateless' that rejected borders and nationhood and operated on a basis of equality and social justice. Even though the local community and local media treated Sophia and Fatih's venture with suspicion and questioned the self-declared independence of the little island state, it did not cause any serious concern beyond the lagoon area. Once refugees – and Bashat in particular – entered the frame, things changed: reports about 'illegal' immigration networks that used the Republic of Baklava as a stepping-stone for entry into the European Union grew; European Border and Coast Guard Agency Frontex moved to the Ionian Sea; Bashat was branded as a 'mysterious trafficker' and the Republic of Baklava a 'terrorist organisation'. After a series of cyber-attacks on Greek government sites and an incident where the Holy Water in Missolonghi's church was 'spiked' with LSD – for both of which Bashat was held responsible – the Greek police and military forces went to Missolonghi and the 'peaceful town with the heroic past [was] under siege again. This time by its own state'. In the end, the police issued an ultimatum for the evacuation of refugees from the island.

If Meze's bullying was the first instance where national(ist) violence became tangible, the arrival of refugees in the Republic of Baklava marked the acceleration of such violence. The presence of refugees on the island seemed to pose a far more serious threat, following Ahmed's phrasing, to 'the border that establishes the "clean body" of the white subject' (2000: 52); a threat not only to Missolonghi or Greece but indeed to the integrity of European borders. In addition, Bashat's radical anti-capitalist politics were far more threatening to the European subject of enunciation than the other Baklavanians, the 'crazy hipster jerks', as per Bashat's description, who made 'more baklava' instead of seizing the opportunity to unsettle the status quo. It was, therefore, the presence of non-white bodies on the island alongside Bashat's radical tactics and politics that produced the Republic of Baklava as that against which Europe could once again re-form its imperial logic.

The different degrees of foreignness – and the unequal exercise of violence against strange bodies – were very clearly articulated in Bashat's intervention during the final assembly of the Republic of Baklava when faced with the police ultimatum to evacuate the refugees. After Fatih proposed to comply and Sophia suggested to 'organise a peaceful demonstration [. . .] and let them come and arrest us all', Bashat reminded them that Fatih, Sophia and the rest of the Europeans could leave the island if they wanted, and this would only have minor implications for their future. 'If we [refugees] surrender right now, they will take us back to a war zone, or to refugee camps under inhumane conditions'. To emphasise this point, Katsis, who was playing Bashat, paused the monologue that was delivered in English and provided in Greek a factual description of refugee camps as places where 'thousands of people share one toilet; [. . .] there is no food; they sleep in tents even when it rains or snows; [. . .] they set themselves on fire because they can no longer stand it and are charged with arson; muggings, rapes, stabbings, black market. Where even the children want to commit suicide'. After this slice of reality, he continued in English: 'This awaits us if we surrender. [. . .] We will fight for our dignity and to set an example. [. . .] Let's face them. Liberty or death'. His argument convinced Baklavanians not to attempt an exodus but to remain and fight, which resulted in the final destruction of the Republic of Baklava.

The mythopoetics of the stranger are indeed unevenly or asymmetrically produced – not all strangers are equally phobic objects. The Baklavanians' decision to fight was, thus, at once an admission of such inequalities and an attempt to overcome them. Their purpose was not to eradicate foreignness but to 'set an example' for a community of de-nationalised subjects, where foreignness is recognised as a fundamental condition of conviviality. In this iteration, the 1821 maxim 'liberty or death' indicated that if these strange bodies could not be equally dignified in life, they might become in their death. In other words, here the revolutionary maxim seems to undo the violence it carries within the scenario of independence – the violence of exclusion – as it calls for an unlearning of the violence of national(ist) history that is at the root of the mythopoetics of the stranger. Thus re-imagined, independence no longer rallied the nation but called for solidarity between strangers who claimed their right to dignity beyond traditions of intolerance that, by and large, are dictated by national(ist) gestures of belonging.

The notion that the Republic of Baklava sought to set an example of a different way of building communities was further supported by the performance's multilingual environment (performers spoke Greek, English, Turkish and German). Each of the four performers spoke at least two languages without trying to mask the fact that they were not native speakers in some of these languages, while they often mixed words from different languages in the same sentence or conversation. Yet, language never became a barrier. The use of multiple languages emphasised specific instances of what Karaoglou calls '"insolent" view on national(ist) myths' – for example, when Solomon spoke in heavily accented Greek as Diakos in the comic book scene.

More importantly, however, the co-existence of different languages and different accents was, to use Katharina Pewny and Tessa Vannieuwenhuyze's phrasing, 'inherently political, for there is nothing neutral about staging the abundant variations of so-called national languages' (2018: 268). By placing the Greek and Turkish (among other) languages next to each other, the performance unsettled the privileged position of the hellenised gaze in the (re)telling of history. In doing so, it reversed a tradition of intolerance that maintains economies of xenophobia by perpetually producing a rhetoric of Greco-Turkish animosity and ring-fencing the national body within the boundaries of the singular enunciation of the national language. As a political gesture, therefore, multilingualism in *The Republic of Baklava* served to de-centre the dominance of the national language and the tyranny of proper enunciation, both symptoms of the nationalisation of communities and, specifically for the case of Greece, a symptom and a means for the Hellenisation of Greeks that, as discussed in Section 1, came at the expense of pre-national multilingual communities that existed in the Balkan peninsula. In line with *The Republic of Balkava's* representation of a de-nationalised political project, multilingualism undid in performative terms the homogeneity of the national body as a way of unlearning the mythopoetics of the stranger that largely operate as a discriminatory mechanism that re-asserts the European colonising gaze.

This de-centring is also evident in the rewinding, as per Azoulay's thinking, of the historic events of the siege and exodus of Missolonghi that emerges in the gaps created by the slippages in its repertoires: the site of resistance had slipped from the city to an island in the lagoon – it had slipped away from the nation's 'sacred' topography of independence, which, in this iteration, became the campsite for the besieging forces; the exodus appeared obsolete and did not take place because the independence fighters were no longer national subjects but strange bodies threatening the national/European body; the besieger was no longer a non-European 'barbarian' army but Europe itself – as represented by the Greek state and Frontex; finally, the nation was no longer an agent of independence but a tyrannical force.

In his review, George Sampatakakis suggests that the performance failed to propose a new way of critiquing xenophobia and nationalism as it remained within well-established performance tropes and posed 'safe protests' within the 'tragic melodrama of heteronormativity' (2022). The point, he argues, is to 'do something subversive, to offer a vital counter-proposal, to protest a violent disassembling rupture and to destroy the core of modern Greek narcissistic gloom in an Artaudian way' (2022). Indeed, *The Republic of Baklava* did not propose a new performance aesthetic – it remained firmly rooted on the tropes of what might be called post-dramatic theatre. Yet, what I propose here is that *The Republic of Baklava*'s key contribution to the critique of the national edifice is far more expansive than the sum of the moments in the performance that parody Greek xenophobia and other national(ist) attitudes: if this re-imagining of independence posed a radical critique, it was because it sought to unlearn the imperial gaze beyond any nostalgia for an 'authentic' and 'pure' pre-national past. It rehearsed, in other words, a gesture of rewinding nationalisation's colonial project at large.

In the performance's coda, Mavrogeorgi presented the final piece of evidence, a letter by little Meze to his dead parents that reached the company 'a few days before opening night'. In this letter, Meze announced that, even though he loved his dead parents, he 'want[ed] to cut all ties with the past', to leave behind both Greece and Turkey as neither 'suits' him anymore. The emotional letter was followed by a baklava-themed rendition of Bonnie Tyler's 'Total Eclipse of the Heart': as if to reconcile the farce and nightmare of history, the ending returned to Paul Valery's words that were uttered by Üzümoglu's rendition of a dying Byron: 'we should not take things as tragic as they are'. Such an ending to the performance seemed to mock the story as much as the medium through which it was told – both the commemoration of the War of Independence and the promise of the documentary. It is precisely by adopting the promise of the documentary and, at the same time, parodying it that this particular iteration of the scenario of independence was able to stage a potential history of contemporary imperial violence, that is, the violence of neoliberal globalisation and its mythopoetics of the stranger. And it was in this sense, that *The Republic of Baklava* rehearsed a de-colonising gesture.

Coda: Performing the National Body

The three examples discussed in the previous sections invited an undoing of the enactment of the scenario of independence as national – a rewinding, that is, of the history of the War of Independence to a time before its nationalisation: before the war was part of a linear movement towards national completion; before Solomos was the National Poet; before foreignness became a 'phobic object'. I have argued that, imbuing the scenario of independence with the history of the present, these productions rehearsed gestures of unlearning of the ways in which the struggle for independence has been colonised by the national gaze and its commemoration continually rehearses the colonisation of the body-politic by the national body. For this, I turn to performances of the national body in this final section: I begin with a brief discussion of the Evzones of the Presidential Guard – which I take to embody the national body *par excellence* – before moving on to discuss the *National Fashion-Show* by Pantelis Flatsousis (Athens Festival, 2021), which, I propose, sought to de-stabilise the ground on which the Evzones rehearse their national repertoires.

Fustanellas and *Evzones*

The March 2021 bicentennial celebrations climaxed with the customary military parade in front of the Greek parliament, of which an important moment was, as per usual, the march of the Presidential Guard: 'While marching, Evzones stomp their tsarouchia [heavy wooden clogs] for the Nation's Unknown dead [soldiers] to hear. Today, as they were leaving the [Unknown Soldier] Monument in absolute silence, their stomping resounded as a Slogan for the new beginning of Hellenism' (@proedrikifroura, 2021). This tweet by the account of the Presidential Guard unmistakably captures the centrality of the Evzone – his body, his ancestry, his physical repertoires and his uniform – to the Greek national imaginary and its repertoires: he is the descendant of the nation's founding fathers, whose attire he still carries; he does not merely commemorate the past, but he initiates the future.

Created in 1868 as 'a combatant and ceremonial elite unit of the Hellenic Army' and after changing names several times, the Greek Presidential Guard is currently a 'purely ceremonial' unit (Presidency of the Hellenic Republic, 2017). Following the examples of other ceremonial military units across Europe, the Evzones's embodied repertoires exhibit strict discipline and training. According to Michel Foucault, '[d]iscipline "makes" individuals; it is the specific technique of a power that regards individuals both as objects and as instruments of its exercises' (1991: 170). The Evzone's body is the exemplary national body because it is a body that has endured the 'means of correct training' as per Foucault's formulation (1991: 170–94). By the same token, and while clearly distinguished from the average body due to its training, the Evzone's body is what Ahmed calls the 'body that appears not to be marked by difference', which holds a 'metonymic relation' to the body-politic, the nation's body (2000: 46). Its repertoires rehearse the body at home as disciplined – 'made' by way of training, as opposed to the wild, savage body of the stranger. The Evzones's repertoires perform the authoritative body of the nation – at once object and instrument of national authority; a docile body that stands in public to discipline the body of the nation.

These disciplinary bodies are dressed in uniforms from the Guard's extant collection of 'traditional' outfits from various regions of Greece: a national archive of sorts at whose heart is the 'Evzone's uniform' whose 'history [. . .] is inextricably linked to Greece's modern history and national identity' (Presidency of the Hellenic Republic, 2017). The Presidential Guard, therefore, operates as the protector of national tradition and, through the ceremonial use of the national dress, its members ostensibly perform the 'bravery and military prowess' of the Greeks (Koulouri, 2020: 411). According to the Presidential Guard's description: the 400 pleats of the fustanella, a white knee-length kilt and arguably the most iconic part of his uniform, 'represent the number of years of the Turkish occupation [sic]'; the fustanella is perceived indiscriminately as the uniform 'of the military leaders and combatants who led the nation's liberation struggles against the Ottomans, during the Greek Revolution of 1821'; whiteness is established as the dominant element of the nation as it 'symbolizes the purity of the struggles for national independence' (Presidency of the Hellenic Republic, 2017).[18] In this framework, the continuity of the fustanella ensures that the transformations of the Presidential Guard are identified with the transformations of the nation-state.

---

[18] The fustanella evolved over the last two centuries from 'everyday attire of some independence fighters and of populations from various regions of the Greek state in the nineteenth century' to 'national dress worn by the head of state [Otto, the first king of Greece], uniform of a military unit of the Greek army, central exhibit in exhibitions and museums, carnival costume and, ultimately, children's toy and tourist attraction' (Koulouri, 2020: 411).

During the twentieth century, fustanella was no longer 'exclusively associated with the Greek Revolution in order to become part of a continuous lineage of "national dresses" that, like everything else, originates in classical antiquity' (Koulouri, 2020: 426). The recognition of 'traditional attire', Koulouri maintains, as 'cultural object is a product of the acceleration of modernity' (2020: 426). In this context, performances of the national body using fustanella contribute to the establishment of a fiction of identity, as per Ulinka Rublack's phrasing (2010: 260), that claims exclusive rights to the heritage of classical antiquity while also following modernity's project of nationalisation. In these processes, fustanella is an essential sign of the nation's representation as extroverted through the commercialisation of its ceremonial use as well as the willingness of European Philhellenes to be pictured wearing it. The Evzones's presence by the unknown soldier, therefore, participates in the tourist ecologies and economies of contemporary Athens, as they attract visitors who wish to photograph them or be photographed alongside them in yet another movement of the imperial shutter. As a ceremonial dress, a metonymy of the nation, fustanella contributes to folklore economies modelled on other European ceremonial guards and performs the 'white purity', discipline and masculinity of the body of the nation – not least because the Presidential Guard consists exclusively of white male bodies of a certain stature. It produces, in other words, the national body as exclusively and irreversibly Hellenic: European, white and masculine.

National Fashion-Show: Undoing the Body of the Nation

In Faltsousis's *National Fashion-Show*, two presenters (George Kritharas and Fotini Papachristopoulou) and five models (Hossain Amiri, Yilmaz Housmen, Deborah Odong, Themis Theocharoglou and Enias Tsamatis) introduced various types of fustanellas and explained who wore them, where and when; sometimes the models enacted the characters who wore them and often they commented on the circumstances. Focusing on the history of the national dress, the show re-imagined the body-politic from a hypothetical vantage point in the year 2121, a time when nation-states no longer exist and there is no theatres and, of course, no fustanellas. Setting the action in 2121 created a temporal distance between the performers/historians in their post-national present and the history they performed; a distance that enabled slippages in the 'choreographies of meaning', to use Taylor's phrasing (2003: 20): as national repertoires belonged to a distant and significantly different past, their repetition was bound to be changed, and as documents were scarce, the dresses differed from their description. Embodied repertoires, dialogues and descriptions emphasised such discrepancies and ambiguities: the performers, for instance, often admitted that they did not know how a dress actually looked like or who exactly wore it or when. By undermining its own attempt to stage the archive convincingly, the *National Fashion-Show* undermined the authority and fixity of the national archive and questioned the very operation of the archive as a durable and complete repository of memory. By re-using texts and garments from the national archive, therefore, the fashion show staged a 'reconstruction of history', as per the director's phrasing, that asked 'whether and how there can be other non-national communities that can promise a more inclusive future – communities that are not based on exclusion' (*CultureNow*, 2021). By troubling, in other words, the national archive, this peculiar fashion show sought to re-dress the future.

Archive trouble was particularly evident in casting choices – critical decisions that, while unearthing hidden voices, sought to undo the body of the nation. The five performers who played the models were, as per Sampatakakis's description, 'a drag queen [Theocharoglou], an immigrant actor [Amiri], a Greek-African female actor [Odong], an important actor born in Albania [Tsamatis] and a star from the "East of Nestos river" [the first Muslim to graduate from the National Theatre's Drama School – Housmen]' (2021). In very different ways, the national, ethnic or gender identity categories of these five performers have experienced exclusions in the context of the nation-state, as critic Matina Kaltaki observes in her review (2021). Theirs were 'strange' bodies, as per Ahmed's discussion, against which the white, masculine and European national body is defined. As such, the performers' embodied repertoires and physicalities failed to conform to the austere masculinity of the *Evzone*, the whiteness of the nationalised subject or the standardised articulation of the singular language.

Two examples may help articulate this point more clearly: at the end of the show, the five models came out onto the catwalk/stage to respond to the question how Greek they felt. Themis Theocharoglou's answer was that during the rehearsals for the show, she felt more Greek and that since he was a little boy, he liked wearing fustanellas – 'it was the only skirt I was allowed to wear'; now she can put it on the way she likes – 'with tights and high heels' (see Figure 9).[19] Despite the clear declaration that she felt Greek to a seven or eight out of ten, the deliberate fluctuation between the male and female pronouns troubled her national identification: the fustanella-wearing body's gender ambiguity seemed to have unlearned the masculine singularity of the national body.

---

[19] The excerpts from the show are sourced from the recording of the performance that Panagiota Konstantinakou, the production's dramaturg, kindly shared with me.

Figure 9 Themis Theocharoglou in *The National Fashion-Show*. Photo Credit:
Michalis Kloukinas

Earlier in the performance, Hossain Amiri recited a passage from the 1822
revolutionary constitution in Farsi; this passage determines that Greek citizens
and non-Greeks who wish to live in Greece must be equal before the law (see
Figure 10). At the end of the passage, he articulated in Greek – speaking with
a recognisably foreign accent – the question that, he proposed, defined state
policies of national identity since 1835: 'Is one born Greek or made one?'
Considering the recent electoral success of the far-right and the legitimisation of
xenophobic rhetoric in public discourse as well as the hostile environment in
which refugees find themselves once they arrive in Greece, such a question
seems very much pertinent in the formation of Greek national bodies.
Nevertheless, as Amiri's non-white body interpreted the 1822 constitution in
his non-European language, he raised questions about multilingualism and
multi-culturalism while also problematising immigration policies beyond the
'exclusion or integration' dilemma.

Rosi argues that '[w]hile spectators watch the parading of the national dress,
the performers' bodies, their "minority voices", offer the audience a diagonal,

Figure 10 Left to right: George Kritharas, Themis Theocharoglou, Hossain Amiri, Deborah Odong and Fotini Papachristopoulou in *The National Fashion-Show*. Photo Credit: Michalis Kloukinas

subversive perspective' (2021). If the national body determines the 'reading' of the national past – and assuming that the audience represents, partly at least, the national body – in the *National Fashion-Show*, the national body looked at its reflection on bodies that the national community always already recognises as strange or as out of place. Nevertheless, strange as those bodies may have been, the five performers/models were not asked to perform themselves as strange or marginalised; rather, their task was to perform models that, while embodying various characters from the Greek history, carried the complexity of their actual identities. In addition, as per Tsamatis's admission, this fashion show was a collective effort that was 'not based on a given text, [but] was co-created' (*TheaterMag*, 2021).[20] As such, these 'strange' bodies walked on the catwalk of history as active agents of a community that was based on ties of solidarity that extended far beyond the national register.

If, as I discussed in Section 1, Delacroix's Greece rehearses the national body as a vulnerable female body who seeks recognition from the European gaze, the

---

[20] It is worth noting here that such decisions in the context of the Athens Festival – which is organised and funded by the Greek state – may appear as tokenistic events (cf. discussion on similar performance events in Jestrovic, 2008). However, in the *National Fashion-Show*, the five models who belong to marginalised identity categories are all professional performers and are employed as such and paid according to relevant legal frames. Moreover, as described here, they are not mere objects in the directorial vision but co-creators of the fashion show.

strange bodies of the *Fashion-Show* seemed to discard such recognition: instead of responding to the dilemma 'is one born Greek or made one', a dilemma that contributes to the reproduction of the national body, the *National Fashion-Show* devised a potential history where the enactment of the scenario of independence is not an exclusive right of the white masculine European body; a potential history that re-imagined the scenario from a point outside of the imperial field of visibility.

The scenario of independence produces the national body as heroic, disciplined and disciplinary: a body that is always already recognised and recognisable – which is known again and anew – as nationalised; a body that performs and reaffirms its nationalisation with each repetition of the scenario. The customary military parade exemplifies such a repetition of the performative reproduction of the national body: as the Evzones and the rest of the military forces march before the national citizenry, they rehearse the scenario of independence while involving the onlookers in the performance's frame. They are performing the nation together, as this commemorative dramaturgy seeks to propose. Yet, such a rehearsal of the nation can only be reductive, formulaic and exclusive; it cannot but fail to take into account the diversity of the body-politic. A Greek military parade is, after all, a white and masculine affair (cf. Hager 2021). It can only commemorate the past as perpetually colonised by the national imaginary; it can only imagine the body-politic as colonised by the imperial gaze.

Contrary to such performances, the examples discussed in this Element rehearsed the scenario of independence in gestures that sought to unlearn the colonisation of the past by the Hellenic ideal; gestures that undid the dichotomy civilisation vs. barbarity; gestures that refused to look at the War of Independence through the movement of the imperial shutter. In doing so, they treated the archive of the nation's birth with insolence and invoked the repertoires of independence only to strip them off the effects of the national tradition. They demonstrated that the archive of independence cannot be settled as it is the archive of a rebellion. Despite any limitations they may have had – and there were limitations when one considers the institutional framework in which they occurred and the audiences they addressed – they troubled the archive of the war by pointing at other histories in which the scenario of independence is complicit; other histories that re-imagine independence by placing the Greek case firmly in its global contexts; by positioning it in the South: Biniaris's *'21* performed a treatise on the meaning of revolution in a time when the discourse of revolution seemed appropriated by neoliberal capitalism – the faceless new father; Efthymiou's *Free Besieged* engaged with the histories of industrialisation and environmental catastrophe in Elefsina, the violent crisis-induced restructuring of the Greek economy before staging their exodus from a post-industrial landscape in a gesture of solidarity; Azas's *The Republic of Baklava* explored the mythopoetics of the stranger – which permeates national encounters with foreignness and which is best exemplified in the treatment of refugees attempting to cross the border into Greece and by extension into Europe – in a gesture that sought to unlearn the knowing again of xenophobia and nationalism and which reveals the nation-state as the perpetrator of barbarism; Flatsousis's *National Fashion-Show*, finally, re-dressed five 'strange' bodies with fustanellas and rehearsed a de-nationalising gesture where the body-politic and the national body were disjointed.

Such adaptations of the scenario of independence are part of a shift in contemporary Greek theatre and performance towards a rewinding of histories that have become 'parched, dead tradition[s]', as per Rosi's phrasing, and that present 'a different understanding of notions of cultural identity and its fluid boundaries' (2021), that is, a shift towards a process of unlearning the nationalisation of political communities. No longer standing in that liminal space between Europe's assumed 'progress' and the Orient's ostensible 'backwardness', they implicate audiences in re-imaginings of independence beyond the field of visibility as determined by the movement of the crypto-colonial shutter. They implicate audiences in a politics of undoing the (self-)colonisation of bodies, cultures and resources. They invite, in other words, spectators to work towards de-colonising the body-politic.

References

@proedrikifroura. (2021). 'While marching, Evzones stomp their tsarouchia for the Nation's Unknown dead to hear. Today, as they were leaving the Monument in absolute silence, the stomping resounded as a Slogan for the new beginning of Hellenism [Οι Εύζωνες κατά τον βηματισμό χτυπούν το τσαρούχι για να ακούνε οι Άγνωστοι νεκροί του Έθνους. Σήμερα κατά την αποχώρησή τους από το μνημείο, η απόλυτη ησυχία που επικρατούσε, το χτύπημα ακουγόταν ως Σύνθημα, για την νέα αρχή του Ελληνισμού]' *Twitter*. 25 March. https://bit.ly/3uN37jP [Accessed 11 November 2022].

Ahmed, S. (2000). *Strange Encounters: Embodied Others in Post-Coloniality*. London: Routledge.

Allard, S. & Côme F. (2018). *Delacroix*. New York: The Metropolitan Museum of Art.

Arendt, H. (2006). *Between Past and Future: Eight Exercises in Political Thought*. New York: Penguin.

Arfara, K. ed. (2016). Scènes en transition: Balkans et Grèce [Scenes in Transition: The Balkans and Greece]. *Théâtre/Public*, 222, 4–115.

Athanassoglou-Kallmyer, N. (1989). *French Images from the Greek War of Independence*. New Haven: Yale University Press.

Azas, A., Bekas, G. & Pitidis, M. (26 July 2021). *The Republic of Baklava* [Play]. Athens Festival, Athens. Performers: Katerina Mavrogeorgi, Cem Yigit Üzümoglu, George Katsis and Gary Salomon. Director: Anestis Azas.

Azoulay, A. A. (2019). *Potential History: Unlearning Imperialism*. London: Verso.

Beaton, R. (2020). *Greece: Biography of a Modern Nation*. London: Penguin.

Belavilas, N., Saiti, T. & Psarioti, K. (2011). *Industrial Heritage in Elefsina and Thriasio Field [Βιομηχανική κληρονομιά στην Ελευσίνα και στο Θριάσιο Πεδίο]*. Athens: Cultural Foundation of Pireos Group.

Benjamin, W. (2003). On the Concept of History. Translated by H. Zohn. In Heiland, H. and Jennings, M. W., eds., *Walter Benjamin: Selected Writings Volume 4 1938–1940*. Cambridge, MA: Belknap Press of Harvard University Press.

Bhabha, H. (1984). Of Mimicry and Man: The Ambivalence of Colonial Discourse. *Discipleship: A Special Issue on Psychoanalysis*, 28, 125–33.

Bhambra, G. K. (2022). A Decolonial Project for Europe. *Journal of Common Market Studies*, 60(2), 229–44.

Biniaris, A. (3 July 2015). *'21* [Play]. Athens Festival, Athens. Performers: Aris Biniaris, Takis Varellas and Vasilis Giaslakiotis. Director: Aris Biniaris.

Boatcă, M. (2021). Thinking Europe Otherwise: Lessons from the Caribbean. *Current Sociology*, 69(3), 389–414.

Boletsi, M. & Papanikolaou, D. (2022). Greece and the Global South: Gestures of spatial disobedience. *Journal of Greek Media and Culture*, 8(2), 129–41.

Boutard (1826). *Fine Arts : Second Exhibition in Favour of the Greeks [Beaux-Arts: Seconde Exposition en Faveur de Grecs]*. In *Journal de Débats*, 2 September 1826.

Calder, D. (2018). *Street Theatre and the Production of Postindustrial Space: Working Memory*. Manchester: Manchester University Press.

Calotychos, V. (2003). *Modern Greece: A Cultural Poetics*. Oxford: Berg.

Cox, E. (2014). *Theatre & Migration*. Basingstoke: Palgrave.

Cox, E. & Zaroulia, M. (2016). Mare Nostrum, or On Water Matters. *Performance Research: A Journal of the Performing Arts* 21(2), In Trubridge, S. (Ed), special issue 'On Sea/At Sea', 141–9.

CultureNow. (2021). *Pantelis Flatsousis on 2121's 'National Fashion-Show'* [*Ο Παντελής Φλατσούσης για το «Εθνικό ντεφιλέ» του 2121!*]. www.culture-now.gr/o-pantelis-flatsoysis-gia-to-ethniko-ntefile-toy-2121-2/ [Accessed 7 November 2022].

Delacroix, E. (1826). *Greece on the Ruins of Missolonghi* [Painting]. Bordeaux: Musée des Beaux-Arts.

Derrida, J. (1998). *Archive Fever: A Freudian Impression*. Translated from French by E. Prenowitz. Chicago: The University of Chicago Press.

Dimadi, I. (2015). *'21, Review. Athinorama*. Last updated: 22 October 2015. https://bit.ly/3FSoh6a [Accessed 13 April 2022].

Dimoula, V. (2018). The Nation Between Utopia and Art: Canonising Dionysios Solomos as the 'National Poet'. In Beaton, R. and Ricks, D., eds., *The Making of Modern Greece*. London: Routledge, pp. 201–10.

Drakopoulou, E. (2021). *Images from the Greek Struggle in European Historical Painting* [Εικόνες του Αγώνα των Ελλήνων στην Ιστορική Ζωγραφική της Ευρώπης]. Athens: Institute of Historical Research/ National Hellenic Research Foundation.

ΕλCulture. (2022). *The Republic of Baklava: Azas's Surrealist Comedy returns in Amphi-Theatro* [Η Δημοκρατία του Μπακλαβά: η Σουρεαλιστική κωμωδία του Ανέστη Αζά επιστρέφει στο Αμφι-Θέατρο]. https://elcultura.gr/i-dimokra tia-tou-baklava-i-sourealistiki-komodia-tou-anesti-aza-gia-liges-parastaseis-sto-amfi-theatro/bit.ly/3Wh5yGP [Accessed 7 November 2022].

Eleusis 2023. (2021a). *Transition to Eu-phoria*. https://bit.ly/3FS8S5T [Accessed 10 February 2022].

Eleusis 2023. (2021b). *Mystery 39: The Free Besieged by Dionysios Solomos, Directed by Eleni Efthymiou.* https://bit.ly/3hxxHL3 [Accessed 10 February 2022].

European Court of Human Rights. (2022). *Safi and Others vs. Greece.* https://bit.ly/3Fqxgu9 [Accessed 11 November 2022].

Flatsousis, P. (26 June 2021). *The National Fashion-Show* [Play]. Athens Festival, Athens. Performers: Hossain Amiri, Yilmaz Housmen, George Kritharas, Deborah Odong, Fotini Papachristopoulou, Themis Theocharoglou and Enias Tsamatis. Director: Pantelis Flatsousis.

Foucault, M. (1991). *Discipline and Punish: The Birth of the Prison.* London: Penguin.

Fragkou, M. (2018). Strange Homelands: Encountering the Migrant on the Contemporary Greek Stage. *Modern Drama*, 61 (3), 301–27.

Gazette de France (1826). *Fine Arts : Painting Exhibition for the Benefit of the Greek [Beaux-Arts: Exposition des Tablaeux aux Profit des Grecs].* In *Gazette de France*, 24 June 1826.

Georgiopoulos, G. (2018). *Greece's Varoufakis Promises to End Debt Bondage with New Party* [Online]. *Reuters.* Last updated: 26 March 2018. https://reut.rs/3YpxOUY [Accessed 30 November 2022].

Gourgouris, S. (2021). *Dream Nation: Enlightenment, Colonization, and the Institution of Modern Greece*, 2nd ed., Stanford, CA: Stanford University Press.

Habermas, J. (2012). *The Crisis of the European Union.* Cambridge: Polity.

Hager, P. (2021). Unstable Histories: Repertoires of Memory and the Making of Public Spheres in Contemporary Greece. *Critical Stages/Scènes Critiques*, 23, Argyropoulou, G. and Sachsenmaier, S., eds., special topic 'Unstable Grounds: Reconfigurations of Performance and Politics'. https://bit.ly/3BwXBoX [Accessed 1 September 2022].

Harvey, D. (2004). The 'New' Imperialism: Accumulation by Dispossession. *Socialist Register 2004: The New Imperial Challenge*, 40, 63–87.

Hatzipantazis, T. (2014). *Outline of a History of Modern Greek Theatre [Διάγραμμα Ιστορίας του Νεοελληνικού Θεάτρου].* Heraklion: Crete University Press.

Hager, P. (2017). Trajectories of Transition: Economies and Geographies of Theatre in Contemporary Athens. *Journal of Greek Media and Culture* 3 (2), In P. Hager and M. Fragkou, eds., special issue 'Dramaturgies of Change: Greek Theatre Now', 139–144.

Hellenic Republic – Prime Minister. (2021). *The PM's Speech at the Opening of the National Gallery [Χαιρετισμός του Πρωθυπουργού Κυριάκου Μητσοτάκη στην εκδήλωση στην Εθνική Πινακοθήκη]* [Video]. https://bit.ly/3HyBtP2 [Accessed 30 May 2022].

Herzfeld, M. (2002). The Absence Presence: Discourses of Crypto-Colonialism. *The South Atlantic Quarterly,* 101(4), 899–926.

Herzfeld, M. (2016). *Cultural Intimacy: Social Poetics and the Real Life of States, Societies, and Institutions.* London: Routledge.

Hobsbawm, E. (1977). *The Age of Revolution 1789–1848.* London: Abacus.

Humboldt, Wilhelm von (1963). *Humanist without Portfolio: an Anthology.* Ed. and trans. Marianne Cowan. Detroit: Wayne State Universtiy Press.

Ioannidou, E. (2011). Toward a National Heterotopia: Ancient Theatres and the Cultural Politics of Performing Ancient Drama in Modern Greece. *Comparative Drama,* 44(4), 385–403.

Jenkins, R. (1940). *Dionysios Solomos.* Cambridge: Cambridge University Press.

Jestrovic, S. (2008). Performing like an Asylum Seeker: Paradoxes of Hyper-Authenticity. *Research in Drama Education,* 13(2), 159–70.

Kairi, E. (2021 [1826]). *Nikiratos [Νηκίρατος].* Athens: Thouli.

Kaltaki, M. (2021). *National Fashion-Show: Greek History and the Development of the National Dress [Εθνικό Ντεφιλέ: Η ελληνική ιστορία μέσα από την εξέλιξη του εθνικού ενδύματος].* Lifo. Last updated: 4 July 2015. https://bit.ly/3ByhBYE [Accessed 30 April 2022].

Kapsomenos, E. (1992b). *Solomos's Text as a Signifying Poetics [Το σωλομικό κείμενο ως σημαίνουσα ποιητική].* In *O Politis* 120, 48–52.

Karaoglou, T. (2022). *The Republic of Baklava, Review [Η Δημοκρατία του Μπακλαβά, Κριτική].* Athinorama. Last updated: 8 February 2022. https://bit .ly/3uPhRyr [Accessed 7 November 2022].

Kasimati, M. Z. (2000). *Athens: Munich: Art and Culture in Modern Greece [Αθήνα – Μόναχο: Τέχνη και Πολιτισμός στη νέα Ελλάδα].* Athens: National Gallery, Museum of Alexadros Soutzos.

Katsikis, I. N. & Tsagkarakis, K. A. (2010). Industries as Urban Cultural Heritage: In Search for a New Use [Η Βιομηχανία ως Αστική Πολιτιστική Κληρονομιά: Σε Αναζήτηση της Νέας Χρήσης]. *Conference Proceedings of the 5th Pan-Hellenic Scientific Meeting TICCIH 'The End of the Giants: Industrial Heritage and Urban Transformations [Το τέλος των γιγάντων: Βιομηχανική κληρονομιά και μετασχηματισμοί των πόλεων]'.* 22–25 November 2007. Volos.

Kitromilides, P. M. (2021). Introduction: In an Age of Revolution. In Kitromilides, P. M. and Tsoukalas, C., eds., *The Greek Revolution: A Critical Dictionary.* Cambridge, MA: Belknap Press of Harvard University Press, pp. 1–15.

Koltsidopoulou, A. (2015). *Liberating Pandemonium [Απελευθερωτικό πανδαιμόνιο]. Kathimerini.* Last updated: 12 July 2015. https://bit.ly /3PrYLrE [Accessed 13 April 2022].

Korais, A. (1814 [2010]). *The Type and Means of Education [Το Είδος και τα Μέσα της Παιδείας]. In Complete Works I [Άπαντα I].* Athens: Vlassis brothers.

Kotides, A. (1995). *Greek Art: Nineteenth Century Painting.* Athens: Ekdotiki Athinon.

Koulouri, C. (2020). *Fustanellas and Togas: Historical Memory and National Identity 1821–1930 [Φουστανέλες και Χλαμύδες: Ιστορική Μνήμη και Εθνική Ταυτότητα 1821–1930].* Athens: Alexandria.

Koumanoudis, I. A. (1845). *Where Does the Art of the Greeks Tread Today [Πού σπεύδει η τέχνη των Ελλήνων σήμερα;].* Belgrade: The Press of the Government.

Laskaris, N. I. (1938–9). *History of Modern Greek Theatre [Ιστορία του Νεοελληνικού Θεάτρου].* Athens: Vasileiou.

Lazzarato, M. (2012). *The Making of the Indebted Man: An Essay on the Neoliberal Condition.* Translated from French by J. D. Jordan. Los Angeles: Semiotext(e).

Mazower, M. (2021). *The Greek Revolution: 1821 and the Making of Modern Europe.* London: Allen Lane.

Mertiri, A. (1993). *Romanticism and Its Impact on the Visual Reality during the Making of the Greek State [Ο Ρομαντισμός και οι διαστάσεις του στην εικαστική πραγματικότητα κατά την διαμόρφωση του νέου ελληνικού κράτους],* Doctoral Thesis. Athens: Department of Political Sciences and International Relations, Panteion University.

Mpalanos, D. S. (1930). *Calendar of Grand Greece [Ημερολόγιον της Μεγάλης Ελλάδος].* Ioannina.

Mparas, P. (2022). *The Republic of Baklava: Azas's Surrealist Comedy's Continued Excitement in Amphi-Theatro [Η Δημοκρατία του Μπακλαβά: η Σουρεαλιστική κωμωδία του Ανέστη Αζά συνεχίζει να ενθουσιάζει στο Αμφι-Θέατρο]. Popaganda.* Last updated: 11 February 2022. https://bit.ly /3WhBVoT [Accessed 7 November 2022].

Mykoniatis, I. (1995). Nineteenth-Century Greek Painting [Η ελληνική Ζωγραφική του 19ου αιώνα]. *Archaeology and the Arts [Αρχαιολογία και Τέχνες],* 57, 6–16.

National Gallery. (2022). *The Exodus from Missolonghi.* https://bit.ly /3UWKQLy [Accessed 20 February 2022].

P. A. (Coupin) (1826). Fine Arts : Painting Exhibition for the Benefit of the Greek [Beaux-Arts: Exposition des Tableaux aux Profit des Grecs]. In *Revue Encyclopédique* 30, 89.

Pagoulatos, G. (2018). *Greece after the Bailouts: Assessment of a Qualified Failure* (GreeSe Papers, 130). London: Hellenic Observatory Discussion Papers on Greece and Southeast Europe, LSE.

Papanikolaou, D. (2017). Archive Trouble, 2017. In Botanova, K., Chryssopoulos, C., Cooiman, J., eds., *Culturescapes: Archaeology of the Future*. Basel: Cristoph Merian Verlag, pp. 38–51.

Pewny, K. & Vannieuwenhuyze, T. (2018). Introduction II: A Laboratory of Diversity. *Modern Drama*, 61 (3), 262–71.

Plantzos, D. (2016). *The Recent Future: Classical Antiquity as a Biopolitical Instrument*. Athens: Nefeli.

Presidency of the Hellenic Republic. 2017. *The Presidential Guard: History and Duties*. https://bit.ly/3uP1qSH [Accessed 5 May 2022].

Prideaux, T. (1966). *The World of Delacroix 1798–1863*. New York: Time-Life Books.

Puchner, W. (2020). *1821 and the Theatre [Το 1821 και το Θέατρο]*. Athens: OTAN.

Reinelt, J. (2009). The Promise of the Documentary. In Megson, C. and Forsyth, A., eds., *Get Real: Documentary Theatre Past and Present*. Basingstoke: Palgrave, pp. 6–23.

Rosi, L. (2021). From History's Archive to the Stage: Contemporary Performances of 1821 [Από το αρχείο της Ιστορίας στη σκηνή του θεάτρου: σύγχρονες παραστάσεις με αφορμή το 1821]. *Hartis [Χάρτης]*, 35, Delveroudi, E. A. ed., special issue '1821 in Theatre and Cinema: representations of the Greek Revolution in Theatre and Cinema [Το 1821 στο θέατρο & στον κινηματογράφο: Αναπαραστάσεις της ελληνικής Επανάστασης στο θέατρο & στον κινηματογράφο]'. https://bit.ly/3PzEYqw [Accessed 30 November 2022].

Rublack, U. (2010). *Dressing up: Cultural Identity in Renaissance Europe*. Oxford: Oxford University Press.

Said, E. (2003). *Orientalism*. London: Penguin.

Sampatakakis, G. (2021a). *Arming the Nation from Behind, National Fashion-Show at the Athens Festival [Αρματώνοντας το έθνος από πίσω, Εθνικό Ντεφιλέ στο Φεστιβάλ Αθηνών]*. Antikritika. Last update: 4 July 2021. https://bit.ly/3BB3H7Y [Accessed 30 April 2022].

Sampatakakis, G. (2021b). From National Panegyrics to Stage Scandal: Athanasios Diakos in History. *Journal of Greek Media and Culture*, 7(2), 281–99.

Sampatakakis, G. (2022). *Banal Pedagogy: The Republic of Baklava in Amphi-Theatro [Μπανάλ παιδαγωγία – Η Δημοκρατία του Μπακλαβά στο ΑΜΦΙ-ΘΕΑΤΡΟ]*. Antikritika. Last update: 11 June 2022. https://bit.ly/3FtshZB [Accessed 30 October 2022].

Santos, B. S. (2020). A New Vision of Europe: Learning from the Global South. In Santos, B. S. and Mendes, J. M., eds., *Demodiversity: Toward Post-Abyssal Democracies*. New York: Routledge, pp. 31–53.

Skaribas, Y. (1995). *1821 and the Truth [To 1821 και η Αλήθεια]*. Athens: Kaktos.

Solomos, D. (25 June 2021). *Mystery 39 The Free Besieged* [Play]. 2023 Eleusis European Cultural Capital. Performers: Myrto Goni, Dimitris Drosos, Ioannis Mastrogiannis, Theodosia Savvaki, Giannis Varvaresos, Maria Antoniou, Maria Axypolitou, Grigoris Asimakopoulos, Thanos Verdis, Angeliki Vlachopanagou, Giannos Gavalas, Athins Gavriilaki, Nikos Galanos, Katerina Gkika, Vanessa Glava, Marina Daskalou, Christos Dedeilias, Anastasia Dracopoulou, Nikolaos Drakoulas, Evangelis Zorzou, Vangelis Kakoseos, Panagiota Kakoseou, Thalia Kallianta, Kyriakos Kabourars, Stavroula Kanaki, Froso Karakitsou, Maria Karelou, Vanassia Katsanebaki, Sotiris Katsanos, Kateirna Koliofoti, Giorgos Kordis, Theodoros Korras, Sophia Linardou, Maria Lioura, Stavros Lourdis, Giannis Marinakis, Natassa Meni, Giorgos Mouroufas, Konstantina Bargiota, Konstantinos Prokopas, Nota Plesti, Paraskevi Papadopoulou, Manolis Papoutsoglou, Natalia Routsolia, Marilena Sabani, Katerina Sarentziotou, Kostas Sidiropoulos, Sotiris Sidiropoulos, Zoi Seitani, Evangelis Totsika, Anastasia Tsoli, Maria Tsoukala, Areti Tsoumani, Pavlina Fourkioti, Maria Chavarioti, Stavros Chanas, Maria Charalambopoulou, Evi Chasioti and Maria Christopoulou. Director: Eleni Efthymiou.

Soutsos, A. (1827). Article in *Friend of the Law [Ο Φίλος του Νόμου]* 266, 7 February.

Stivanaki, E. (2000). Evanthia Kairi's Patriotic Play *Nikiratos* [Ο πατριωτικός Νικήρατος της Ευανθίας Καΐρη]. *Paravasis [Παράβασις]*, 3, 257–71.

Tabaki, A. (1993). *Modern Greek Playwriting and its Western Influences (18th–19th Centuries): A Comparative Approach [Η Νεοελληνική Δραματουργία και οι δυτικές της επιδράσεις (18ος -19ος αι.): Μια συγκριτική προσέγγιση]*. Athens: Tolidis.

Tabaki, A. (1997). Enlightenment and Romanticism in Modern Greek theatre [Ο Διαφωτισμός και ο Ρομαντισμός στο Νεοελληνικό Θέατρο]. In *Modern Greek Theatre 17th–20th Century: Scholarly Educative Talks [Νεοελληνικό Θέατρο 17ος – 20ος Αιώνας: Επιστημονικές Επιμορφωτικές Διαλέξεις]*. Athens: ΕΙΕ, pp. 37–58.

Tabaki, A. (2021a). The 1821 Revolution in the Theatre: The Case of Ioannis Zambelios [Η Επανάσταση του 1821 στο θέατρο. Η περίπτωση του Ιωάννη Ζαμπέλιου]. *Proceedings of the 10th International Conference for the 200*

Years from the Greek Revolution, 'The Impact of 1821 in Literature and the Arts'. 27–28 November 2020, Athens. Athens: Archontariki.

Tabaki, A. (2021b). Introduction. In *Nikiratos ... the Path to Freedom: Based on the play Nikiratos by Evanthia Kairi* [Νικήρατος ... ο δρόμος για την Ελευθερία, βασισμένο στο θεατρικό έργο «Νικήρατος» της Ευανθίας Καΐρη]. Athens: Dromon, pp. 29–40.

Taylor, D. (2003). *The Archive and the Repertoire: Performing Cultural Memory in the Americas.* Durham, NC: Duke University Press.

TheaterMag. (2021). *Enias Tsamatis. As Kapodistrias, as Kolettis in the 'National Fashion-Show'* [Αινείας Τσαμάτης. Ως Καποδίστριας, ως Κωλέττης στο «Εθνικό Ντεφιλέ»]. Last update: 24 June 2021. www.theatermag.gr/2021/06/24/aineias-tsamatis-os-kapodistrias-os-kolletis-sto-ethniko-defile/.

Tsatsoulis, D. (2015). *Liberty Is the Work of the Devil* [Έργον Διαβόλου η Ελευθερία]. *Imerodromos* [Ημερόδρομος]. Last update: 6 July 2015. https://bit.ly/3W1SXrq [Accessed 4 January 2022].

Tsatsoulis, D. (2017). *Western Hegemonic Paradigm and Intercultural Theatre* [Δυτικό Ηγεμονικό Παράδειγμα και Διαπολιτισμικό Θέατρο]. Athens: Papazisis.

Tsoukalas, C. (2021a). On National Anniversaries: Greece, 1821–2021. *Journal of Balkan and Near Eastern Studies*, 23(2), 181–98.

Tsoukalas, K. (2021b). Symbolic Commemorations and Cultural Affiliations. In Kitromilides, P. M. and Tsoukalas, C., eds., *The Greek Revolution: A Critical Dictionary.* Cambridge, MA: Belknap Press of Harvard University Press, pp. 708–24.

Tziovas, D. (1999). The Reception of Solomos: National Poetry and the Question of Lyricism. *Byzantine and Modern Greek Studies*, 23(1), 164–94.

Tziovas, D. (2003). *Greece and the Balkans: Identities, Perceptions and Cultural Encounters since the Enlightenment.* London: Routledge.

Tziovas, D. (2014). *The Illusive Continuity* [Η απατηλή συνέχεια]. *To Vima* [Το Βήμα]. 16 February 2014, A51.

Tziovas, D. (2021). *Greece from Junta to Crisis Modernization, Transition and Diversity.* London: I.B Tauris.

Van Steen, G. (2015). *Stage of Emergency: Theater and Public Performance under the Greek Military Dictatorship of 1967–1974.* Oxford: Oxford University Press.

Van Steen, G. (2021). Anniversaries. In Kitromilides, P. M. and Tsoukalas, C., eds., *The Greek Revolution: A Critical Dictionary.* Cambridge, MA: Belknap Press of Harvard University Press, pp. 694–707.

Varoufakis, Y. (2016). *And the Weak Must Suffer What They Must? Europe, Austerity and the Threat to Global Stability.* London: Vintage.

Vasilaki, R. & Souvlis, G. eds. (2021). *Normalisation of Alt-Right Rhetoric in Greece: Gender, Media, Armed Forces, Church* [*Η Κανονικοποίηση του Ακροδεξιού Λόγου στην Ελλάδα: Φύλο, ΜΜΕ, Ένοπλες Δυνάμεις, Εκκλησία*]. Athens: Rosa Luxemburg Institute – Greek Branch.

von Hess, P. (1852). *The Arrival Otto, First King of Greece, in Nafplio on February 6 1833*. Lithograph, National Historical Museum, Athens.

Vryzakis, T. (1853). *The Exodus from Missolonghi* [Painting]. Athens: National Gallery.

Vryzakis, T. (1861). *The Reception of Lord Byron at Missolonghi* [Painting]. Athens: National Gallery.

Zaroulia, M. & Hager, P. (2014). Europhile or Eurosceptic? Gaps in the Narrative and Performances of Panic. In Tsilimpounidi, M. and Walsh, A., eds., *Remapping 'Crisis': A Guide to Athens*. Winchester, DC: Zero Books, pp. 226–47.

Acknowledgements

As any other piece of scholarly work, this Element is a collective effort. It is through the generosity and thoughtfulness of others that the ideas and arguments presented in the following pages were developed.

First, I am grateful to the series editors Liz Tomlin and Trish Reid for their invitation, feedback and patience. I am also indebted to the anonymous reviewer whose comments have helped me clarify and nuance my thinking. Dear friends and colleagues Eleftheria Ioannidou, Ally Walsh and Lina Rosi read drafts of this Element, and I thank them for their time and valuable comments. The idea for this Element came out of thoughts I first presented in a short post on the 2021 celebrations for the Greek bicentennial that was part of the 'Greek Studies Now' blog. I am thankful to the editorial team (Maria Boletsi, Dimitris Papanikolaou, Kristina Gedgaudaitė, Yiorgos-Evgenios Douliakas, Claudio Russello and Periklis Douvitsas) for the space they provided as well as their comments. Furthermore, some of the work included here was first presented at the 'Performance: Theory and Practice' conference (Patras, Greece, April 2022) and the 'Nation, Gender, Politics of Identity in Performing Arts and Cinema' symposium (Patras, Greece, May 2022). These events were important for the development of my work, and I thank the organisers and delegates.

Eleni Efthimiou, Anestis Azas and Panagiota Konstantinakou kindly shared documentation and took the time to discuss their work with me, for which I am grateful. I am also grateful to the National Gallery of Greece for kindly allowing me to use images of the two paintings by Theodoros Vryzakis and specifically to photographer Stavros Psiroukis and the National Gallery's director Syrago Tsiara. I also wish to thank the Athens and Epidaurus Festival and Dimitra Kondylaki, Eleusis 2023 Cultural Capital of Europe and the photographers Pinelopi Gerasimou, Michalis Kloukinas, Evi Fylaktou and Angelos Christophilopoulos who kindly gave me permission to use their photographs.

Finally, I want to thank my partner, Marissia Fragkou, whose contribution to this Element cannot be put in words.

Cambridge Elements $\equiv$

Theatre, Performance and the Political

Trish Reid
University of Reading
Trish Reid is Professor of Theatre and Performance and Head of the School of Arts and Communication Design at the University of Reading. She is the author of *The Theatre of Anthony Neilson* (2017), *Theatre & Scotland* (2013), *Theatre and Performance in Contemporary Scotland* (2024) and co-editor of the *Routledge Companion to Twentieth-Century British Theatre* (2024).

Liz Tomlin
University of Glasgow
Liz Tomlin is Professor of Theatre and Performance at the University of Glasgow. Monographs include *Acts and Apparitions: Discourses on the Real in Performance Practice and Theory* (2013) and *Political Dramaturgies and Theatre Spectatorship: Provocations for Change* (2019). She edited *British Theatre Companies 1995–2014* (2015) and was the writer and co-director with Point Blank Theatre from 1999–2009.

About the Series
Elements in Theatre, Performance and the Political showcases ground-breaking research that responds urgently and critically to the defining political concerns, and approaches, of our time. International in scope, the series engages with diverse performance histories and intellectual traditions, contesting established histories and providing new critical perspectives.

Cambridge Elements ≡

Theatre, Performance and the Political

Elements in the Series

Theatre Revivals for the Anthropocene
Patrick Lonergan

Re-imagining Independence in Contemporary Greek Theatre and Performance
Philip Hager

A full series listing is available at: www.cambridge.org/ETPP